"*Letters from a Tiger Mom*  speak to the essence of parenting. Ann Yabusaki poses reflection questions that artfully allow you to view your experiences and challenge you in a way that can lead to greater unconditional love and transformation. An insightful book for conscious parents."

—Marci Shimoff,
#1 *New York Times* bestselling author,
Happy for No Reason and *Chicken Soup for the Woman's Soul*

"*Letters from a Tiger Mom* is an insightful book for conscientious parents who would heed their call against the backdrop of a deadening culture-specific neurosis of longstanding: Asian American families that raise their offspring in terms of what Karen Horney called 'the tyranny of the should.'"

—Benjamin R. Tong, PhD,
Emeritus Professor of clinical psychology,
California Institute of Integral Studies; founding faculty, Asian American Studies Department, San Francisco State University.

"A candid and easy-to-read book on real parenting with its ups and downs that many of us parents will easily relate to. Take the time to read this if you are a parent or are interested in being one. You'll enjoy the author's personal stories and perspectives on parenting."

—Jackie Hong, parent and retired social worker

"*Letters from a Tiger Mom* gives great interactive question pages, presents genuine honesty in poetic clothing, and is a wonderful opportunity for empathic learning. This book is a gift to every parent who will read it ... especially those who were once children themselves."

—Dr. Robert F. Morgan,
author of *Time Statues* and *Time Statues Revisited*

"A deeply insightful and refreshingly honest reflection on parenting. Ann's heartwarming letters to her children are punctuated with laughter, tears, and love. As Ann shares her own parenting journey and her insights along the way, she masterfully leads the reader to reflect on their own parenting."

—Karen Pratten,
CEO Emotional Keys, Happy for No Reason Certified Trainer

"In *Letters from a Tiger Mom*, Ann describes courageously and honestly her journey as a parent of two children, from birth to young adulthood. Some stories she tells would turn any parent's hair white. Ann's love of learning compelled her and her husband to reassess their assumptions, eventually finding a place of harmony with their children. Ann takes a multi-generational approach, discovering how families of origin impacted her family in unique and hidden ways."

—Roberta Stephens, policy analyst

"*Letters from a Tiger Mom* is an invitation to share a mother's unique heart song. Dr. Ann reflects candidly upon her own journey as a parent, from acknowledged angst to unconditional love. Her personal and professional insights offer the reader an invaluable opportunity for self-reflection and conscious growth. *Letters* is a cultural memoir and gift book for Dr. Ann's adult children. It is also a wisdom book for every parent."

—Dianne Poole,
retired RN, Hospice of Martha's Vineyard

"In this well-written and well-organized book, Ann chronicles the joys and challenges of raising a son and daughter, the son the elder, the adopted from Korea daughter the younger. All of this takes place against two Japanese cultural backgrounds, Ann's Okinawan-Japanese-Hawaiian majority and her husband Ken's mainland Japanese presence that was regarded as hostile in the USA; Ken's people were interred in northern Idaho during the war. Any parent will recognize and profit from the tensions and their resolutions described, best be described by what could be an alternate title of the book, love conquers all."

—Joe K. Fugate, PhD,
Kalamazoo College emeritus

"A courageous trek into the complicated longitudinal journey of parenthood, Yabusaki demonstrates how love and a willingness to learn from our children can be transformative. She reveals the raw turbulent confusion she experienced, which, even as a highly educated family therapist, she was at times unable to connect with her children. She also shows how being a life-long student of human philosophies and cultures led her to be at peace with being a good enough person and mom. Wisdom is within these pages!"

—Susana Ming Lowe, PhD,
psychologist

"In *Letters from a Tiger Mom*, Ann Yabusaki reveals her heartfelt, insightful journey to face in herself the actual impact she had on her children from her beliefs about families and perfection. Her courageous descriptions create an intimate, safe environment for readers to consider the questions she offers, each one from her own transformative path to unconditional love. Help yourself!"

—Miriam Goldberg, PhD

LETTERS FROM A TIGER MOM

LETTERS FROM A TIGER MOM

A Protective Mother's Reflections
on Parenting Strong-Willed Children

Ann S. Yabusaki, PhD

Copyright © 2023 Ann S. Yabusaki, PhD

All rights reserved. No part of this book may be used or reproduced or transmitted in any form or by any means whatsoever, including electronic or mechanical, photocopying, recording, or by any information storage and retrieval system, without the written permission of the publisher. For information, contact ayabusaki2@gmail.com.

This book is not to be used as a substitute for medical treatment, psychotherapy, or another health program of any nature. If you choose to follow any of the techniques offered in this book, you willingly and knowingly shall bind yourself, the members of your family or those living with you, and anyone impacted by your actions to not hold the author or those associated with the book as responsible for any and all risks, injuries, or damages that may have incurred from your actions and decision to follow any advice, information, or direction provided within the book.

Production & Publishing Consultant: Geoff Affleck AuthorPreneur Publishing Inc.—authorpreneurbooks.com
Editor: Nina Shoroplova—ninashoroplova.ca
Cover Designer: pagatana.com
Interior Designer: Amit Dey—amitdey2528@gmail.com

ISBN: 979-8-9875210-0-7 (paperback)
ISBN: 979-8-9875210-1-4 (eBook)
ISBN: 979-8-9875210-2-1 (audiobook)

FAM032000 FAMILY & RELATIONSHIPS / Parenting / Motherhood
FAM033000 FAMILY & RELATIONSHIPS / Parenting / Parent & Adult Child
BIO021000 BIOGRAPHY & AUTOBIOGRAPHY / Social Scientists & Psychologists

For Ken, my husband and partner in parenting;
and to my teachers, Sean and Lee,
parents, grandparents, and ancestors.
Okage sama de. ("I am what I am because of you.")

CONTENTS

Preface xv

Introduction xix

PART ONE: A LETTER TO MY SON 1

Reflection 1: Trust the Universe. 5

Reflection 2: My Children Show Me How to Parent. 7

Reflection 3: It's Never Too Early to Begin Engaging with
My Child 12

Reflection 4: My Child Trusts His Gut and I Can Too 15

Reflection 5: I Learn My Child's Language. 19

Reflection 6: Nurturing the Spirit of My Children—It Will
Get Them through Life 26

Reflection 7: Children Discover Themselves in Many Ways . . 31

Reflection 8: Letting Go 34

PART TWO: A LETTER TO MY DAUGHTER 39

Reflection 9: Never Assume What Is False to Be True 43

Reflection 10: I Learned Patience Over the Years in Bonding
with My Child 48

Reflection 11: Picking My Battles to Win the War. 53

Reflection 12: Letting Go Is an Art, Not a Science, So I'm
	Trusting My Gut 59
Reflection 13: There Is No Such Thing As Taking a Break
	from Parenting 63
Reflection 14: Sometimes, the Best Way to Teach Is Through
	"Natural Consequences". 67
Reflection 15: The Mediated Learning Experience Saved
	My Sanity 70
Reflection 16: Keep the Lines of Communication Open . . . 78

**PART THREE: IT'S IMPOSSIBLE TO PROTECT
	MY CHILDREN FROM THE WORLD 93**

Reflection 17: While We Tried to Protect You, Our Children 97
Reflection 18: About the Past Being the Present. 100
Reflection 19: Developing a Parental View is Critical. 105
Reflection 20: My Life of Embracing a Cultural Identity
	Is As Challenging As a Caterpillar Becoming
	a Butterfly. 109
	Childhood Years 109
	College Years .110
	My Junior Year Abroad 113
	Graduate School 116
	Nothing Prepared Me for Parenting in a
	Different Culture 116
Reflection 21: My Grandparents and Parents 119
	Your Hawaii Great-Grandparents 119
	Your Hawaii Grandma's Story. 122
	Your Hawaii Grandpa's Story 124

Reflection 22: Your Grandpa in Hawaii 127
    Fierce Independence Is Necessary for Living
    a Successful Life 127
    Children Are Gold 128
    Cultural Protocols Are Important 129
    Parenting Is Challenging in Any Language . . 133
Reflection 23: Your Dad's Experience of Hawaii 135
Reflection 24: Your Seattle Grandparents' Story 138

PART FOUR: LETTING YOU GO REQUIRES COURAGE . . 143
Reflection 25: The Final Exam of Parenting 145
Reflection 26: Children Find Their Path in Their Own Ways . . 148
Reflection 27: Growing My Self 150
Reflection 28: Despite Our Wishes, We Need to Let Go . . . 152
Reflection 29: A Nightmare Might Have Been a Blessing . . . 155
Reflection 30: Setting Our Limits Helped 158
Reflection 31: When Your Opponent Pushes, Step Aside . . . 160
Reflection 32: Deliberately Creating Love Experiences 163
Reflection 33: Never Give Up—The Truth Emerges 166
Reflection 34: Love Prevails 170

PART FIVE: MY CHILDREN HAVE TAUGHT ME MORE
THAN I HAVE TAUGHT THEM 173
My Transformation 175
Have Compassion for Yourself As a Parent 178

Acknowledgments 183
About the Author 185

PREFACE

This book came from fragments of conversations my husband and I had with our adult children. On one occasion, our adult children and teenage grandchildren came to our home for dinner. My husband and I enjoyed and continue to enjoy these evenings, as we inevitably share stories and memories of our family.

What our children said often surprised me and piqued my curiosity, leaving me fascinated by what they remember and how they view their childhoods. This way I learn a lot about what's important to them now.

One evening our son commented, "My friends say they wish they had the kind of relationships we have as a family."

I was shocked and asked, "Huh? Why?"

He shrugged and casually explained, "I think it's because we don't fight and argue. They don't want to visit their parents because they usually end up disagreeing about something, and they end up leaving angry."

At another dinner, our son declared, "I had a great childhood," and when I asked him what he meant, he said, "I felt free and happy! It was great!"

I watched his infectious smile light up his face, and I guessed he was recalling some happy memories. At that moment, I saw him as the child we raised, a child who lived with a wildly expansive heart that refused to be tamed. I could only reflect that this child lived from his soul; I didn't see that when he was younger.

On another occasion, our daughter said, "I don't want my kids doing what I did!" And later, she said, "I'm glad they were not like me when I was their age. I feel so lucky my kids are not on drugs."

The children's memories were so different from mine. Many of mine were of my being a hysterical, out-of-control mom, trying to reason with her children to behave and not make us look like bad parents and not shame the family. My husband and I often remembered the parenting journey as a push and pull—they pushed us, we pulled, and they were always just out of reach. I have wondered whether children grow into themselves from the force of pushing and pulling against their parents.

I wrote this book hoping to make sense of what the parenting experience was about and perhaps pass some wisdom about life on to the children. We seemed to have experienced many events very differently, and now that they are adults and parents themselves, and have worked with children, as our son did at a private high school, I thought our story might help them to understand the role of adults in a child's life. While writing, however, my stories and memories started to take a new perspective. I learned that my parenting experience was about me—not about my children or our family life. The parenting journey was about learning to listen to and hear my children, honoring their souls, and learning about the purpose of parenting.

Preface

I never dreamed parenting would be so challenging and rewarding; seeing our children as happy, self-sufficient, kind, and loving people warms my heart. Because of them, I realize that I did not have the answers to make them happy. They had the answers within themselves. I needed to stand by as they tried to find their voices and their way in the world, to catch and pick them up when they fell down, and simply love them.

Now I realize that I wrote this book to thank and remind them how much they taught me and how much they were loved. And when I shared drafts of this book with them, they encouraged me to continue. They loved the memories and enjoyed reliving our journey as a family!

INTRODUCTION

Ma ka hana ka 'ike
"The knowledge is in the doing."

(Hawaiian Olelo No'eau or Proverb)

Unless you "show up," you don't know what can happen. I am a perfectionist. I love to plan, organize, and prepare for every conceivable wrinkle in the unforeseen future. So, when I got pregnant, I studied about babies, child development, parenting strategies, theories, and what to expect so I wouldn't have any surprises. I was confident my children would automatically be model kids and responsible adults.

What a joke. I was never so humbled.

I never dreamed that becoming a parent would put me through such a washing machine of feelings. I tumbled, spun, respun, reversed the spin cycle, and on many days, I just felt dizzy and completely helpless. And I was never done.

My parenting became a prayer and an act of faith.

Dealing with the bodies of little people with minds of their own who want to experiment and live life their own way and are willing to expose their parents' inadequacies and embarrass them in surprisingly creative ways is like holding on to water. And yet we love our children no matter how much they fail, yell, and scream, or we ground them. No matter how much I planned, my plans didn't work.

I learned from my children that nothing could prepare me for parenting.

This book is about my personal journey in parenting. As a family therapist and psychologist with over forty years of practicing in the mental health field, with countless hours of meditation, self-improvement workshops, and spiritual journeys to improve my parenting, I finally conceded that the theories of mental health and family therapy do not always translate into solutions.

The ultimate lesson I learned from parenting was to cultivate compassion for myself.

In our family, my husband and I have encountered tremendous challenges but, in retrospect, these challenges were lessons, and these lessons turned out to be miracles ... even though I might not have recognized them as precious gifts at the time.

Our son brought us profound awe for life with his conception and birth. Our daughter brought us immense respect for the human spirit when, aged nearly three years old, she stepped off the plane from Korea and moved into our lives.

I felt a deep love immediately for both our children, and I joyfully accepted the responsibility for these gifts of life. As we journeyed together with our new family, my husband and I often discussed how best to handle difficult situations and, after each trying episode, we felt a more profound commitment to our children.

Introduction

Through my children, I have experienced deep joy, happiness, anger, frustration, love, surprises, disappointment, and moments of awe. I learned to let go of my sometimes perfectionist need for control and instead to trust the universe. As I worried about and tried to foster a sense of self-confidence in the children themselves, I realized I was teaching them, as well, to embrace self-love.

I have also learned that clinging to them resulted in their pushing back and forcing me to see I needed to let them go. I learned to confront my ego, raise myself up to unconditional love, forgive myself for my many mistakes in raising them, and give thanks for a level of patience and love that I would never have known without them.

I invite you to join me on my journey of parenting. The journey forced me out of my comfort zone into being a parent, a better person, a friend, a partner, and a therapist. Our children showed me the meaning of unconditional love.

There are five parts to this book with reflection chapters in each part. After reading each of the chapters, I invite you to reflect on your experiences and how the parenting experience might have influenced or transformed you. I wish you many wonderful stories and profound reflections as you grow with your children.

PART ONE

A LETTER TO MY SON

*Being deeply loved by someone gives you strength,
while loving someone gives you courage.*

Lao Tzu

My Dearest Sean,

Your birth was a miracle that hit me like a bolt of lightning. When you were born, I felt a surge of love and a purpose for life that I'd never felt before. Your dad and I were so excited about seeing you and holding you, a child we had only known in the womb.

Nothing prepared me for your arrival, despite all my studying about birth and infancy. It was mind-boggling to me when I first saw you, a wrinkled, pink, tiny creature squirming in my arms. Your eyes were tightly closed and you stretched and yawned with tiny clenched fists.

My first thought was, *Oh, my God! What have we done? What is this thing? Who is this person we're supposed to care for?*

As you nestled into my body, I felt an overwhelming sense of Divine Love—love in a way I had never experienced before. All I could say was, "Thank you! Thank you!" My feelings overwhelmed me, and I knew that you were and are a gift from

God. As you suckled at my breast, I felt a connection to all goodness. Words escaped me.

With this Love, your dad and I vowed to be your fiercest guardians and protectors. No one would hurt you, and we promised always to support you.

YOUR TURN TO REFLECT

Recall the first moment you laid eyes on your child. What did you experience?

REFLECTION 1

TRUST THE UNIVERSE

You walked unsteadily at eight months and ran by twelve months. I loved watching you run to your dad with open arms when he arrived home walking his bicycle down the sidewalk toward our apartment. You wore little blue *tabis* (Japanese socks) and a light blue sweater as you ran with your huge, infectious smile, laughing in pure delight with the hugs and kisses from your dad. I saw a boy who loved his father, and your passion for him made me love him even more.

Your love was contagious.

As you grew, you showed no fear—you embraced life. If you had a mantra, it would have been "Trust the Universe."

I learned the courage to love from you.

I would have to revisit this unconditional love often as you and your sister challenged us to let each of you grow in your own ways.

YOUR TURN TO REFLECT

Did your child's love of your partner deepen your love for him or her more? I invite you to revisit that moment often to know the depth of Love.

— REFLECTION 2 —

MY CHILDREN SHOW ME HOW TO PARENT

When you, Sean, were still an infant, our pediatrician suggested that we allow you to cry yourself to sleep so you could learn how to soothe yourself.

That night, after bathing, nursing, cuddling, and singing to you, your dad and I put you in your crib and walked out of your room. My heart ached as I listened to your cries and I wanted to rush in to comfort you.

After a few days of this, you slept without crying. I was amazed and wondered when and how I could learn to step back and trust that you would learn what you needed to learn by yourself and still be safe … not just for these nights but throughout the rest of your life.

Soon you showed me more about what you could do. When you were eleven months old, I took you to a babysitter weekly while I attended university classes. The sitter lived nearby, in the same apartment complex as us, so you and I walked to and from her place. One day your babysitter and I sat and chatted for a few minutes, and when I turned to get you to walk home, you were gone. I had mistakenly left her front door open. I ran out, looking up and down the walkways for you.

I couldn't find you, and I panicked. How could I have lost you? I ran out of her apartment and retraced our usual route home. When I arrived at our apartment, you were sitting on the cement steps at the front door. You had walked home in your diapers and a t-shirt, and were patiently waiting for me.

I realized then that you had a keen sense of observation. You had already absorbed everything about our little neighborhood.

This next period of development was a tremendous learning curve for me—as well as for you—while you taught me how much more children know than I thought they did. That was something I could never have learned from my school studies.

When Dad and I hired our first babysitter for a date night, you were about a year old. When the babysitter arrived that night (and every time after that when we announced that she had arrived to take care of you), you would immediately grab your purple blanket from the couch, trot off to your room, lie down on your sleeping bag, close your eyes, and fall asleep. We'd tuck you in and kiss you good night, and you somehow willed yourself to fall asleep … immediately. I was fascinated with your ability to fall asleep so quickly and so easily. I never knew how or why you did it. I even guessed that maybe you didn't like babysitters. You never complained about the babysitter, but you would always go to your sleeping bag and fall asleep, sometimes even before she arrived.

You only spoke a few words in those days, but you insisted that we learn your language. For example, you said, "mi" to me one morning (it sounded like the word *me*) and you pointed to the water faucet. I remember I wasn't sure at first what you meant, but I gave you some water and realized that when you took it and drank it, "mi" meant water.

We knew *mizu* (pronounced *meezoo*) means water in Japanese, but we didn't speak Japanese around you. Dad and I wondered why you called water "mi." We had never heard "mi" before.

One day I thought it was time you learned "water" so that others could understand you. I squatted in front of you, holding a glass of water. I pointed to the water and said, "Wa …"

You said, "Wa …"

I said, "… ter."

You said, "… ter."

I smiled broadly and said, "Water!"

You said, "Mi!" Then you burst out laughing.

I was amazed to learn that you had such a sense of humor at twelve months and enjoyed playing jokes. You taught me that children are clever and determined from a very young age.

Your imagination and ability to solve problems continue to amaze your dad and me, even today.

At that time, of course, I wasn't aware how much that creative mind of yours would later challenge us in our efforts to parent you.

I always encouraged you to take time out for yourself to develop a capacity to rest, to enjoy being with your thoughts and heart, and to create a meditation or a "quiet" time for yourself. For the first five years of your life, I always insisted that you nap or have quiet time. Initially, you napped and awoke refreshed. Later, you would go to your room to play quietly with your toys. You built cities, airplanes, monsters, and animals with your Lego sets, and made up fantastic stories about your creations during those quiet moments. You once said that these were some of the best times in your life. We had no idea how your powers of concentration, focus, and imagination would carry you throughout your life.

As you grew up, I know I tended to worry a lot, but I didn't realize what a burden my worry was to you. Once, exasperated—you were twelve at the time—you finally said to me, "Mom, stop worrying! You're undermining my self-confidence!"

I learned from you that my role was to give you the space and time to explore and nurture your own innate wisdom and to not let my own fears interfere with your growth.

YOUR TURN TO REFLECT

When did you discover that your child had a personality and mind of their own?

_____

_____

_____

_____

_____

_____

_____

What was that experience like for you?

_____

_____

_____

_____

_____

_____

_____

———— REFLECTION 3 ————

IT'S NEVER TOO EARLY TO BEGIN ENGAGING WITH MY CHILD

I wasn't sure if you could even focus your eyes at two months old, so I decided that I'd tell you about this world. I was excited to share my world with you. I propped you on a blanket in a rickety, orange, plastic, infant carrier, placed it on the kitchen floor so you could safely watch me, and explained everything to you that I was doing.

I demonstrated how to measure ingredients, describing the items I used to make a meal; I showed you how to stir or cut food and to toss salads, and I explained why you should follow an ordered sequence when making meals.

I always cooked a meal with a precise plan; it never occurred to me that someone else might not.

I showed you knives, spoons, measuring cups, bowls, pots, and pans and explained how to use them. I showed you fruit, vegetables, and meat, telling you their names and how to prepare and cook each for meals. Your eyes followed me wherever I went, and you seemed to listen and smile as I prattled on about preparing meals. You waved your tiny fists and kicked your chubby legs—as if to stretch and learn about your body—and that encouraged me to continue.

You seemed to enjoy our kitchen demonstrations and I enjoyed teaching you. I laughed and giggled with you, imitating and tickling you throughout our time together in the kitchen. I had no idea what you were learning, but I thought you might soon discover words.

I didn't realize then that in those hours together, we might have taught each other how to do a certain kind of dance, how to laugh, understand, and speak our unspoken, unique language.

As you grew, I saw that you were a great listener, a keen observer, and someone who could focus and concentrate for hours on tasks that interested you. Because of you, in my practice, I now teach parents the lesson of modeling, playing, and engaging infants early on.

YOUR TURN TO REFLECT

What was it like when your infant first smiled and acknowledged you?

REFLECTION 4

MY CHILD TRUSTS HIS GUT AND I CAN TOO

At age three, you and your best friend, Geoffrey, would play together for hours. I often watched you walk confidently past the utility building and down the walkway to the end of the next apartment complex to your best friend's apartment. You spent hours there, coming home only to eat and nap. You loved playing with him, and when you were finally tall enough, you would reach up on tiptoe to grab the front doorknob and yell, "I'm going to Jiffy's!"

I could barely keep up with you.

By age four, you became part of a Big Wheels "gang" of four. Your plastic wheels ground noisily against the sidewalk as you four sped through the complex yelling ... four soldiers fighting an imaginary villain and laughing about it throughout the day.

I didn't realize that the neighbors were upset with the noise until someone posted a sign in the laundry room that children could not ride their Big Wheels before eight a.m. on Sunday mornings. I had been so impressed with your motor and verbal skills, your ability to socialize, and your overall development that I had neglected to think that others might think of the noise as a nuisance.

One day, while I was in our bedroom office transcribing an audiotape from my boss, you ran wide-eyed into our apartment. You showed me a cut on your head, and I immediately rushed to clean and dress it.

"What happened?" I asked as I patched you up.

"Me and Curly," you explained—he was a member of your Big Wheels gang—"were playing outside when Soso and Robitussin threw a can and it hit my head."

Upset, I asked, "Why did they throw the can?"

"Me and Curly were playing 'statue' when Soso and Robitussin threw it."

I saw the problem had come from playing "statue."

"Curly and you may have scared Soso and Robitussin," I said, "when you didn't talk or move, playing statue."

I patched you up and told you to apologize to them. You ran out the door again. Later I saw you and Curly back playing with Soso and her brother, Robitussin.

What else was there for me to say? You learned a lesson about people and were honest with your friends about what happened. I never wanted you to regret telling the truth, and I understood then that you could learn from your experiences.

I also saw that we had better conversations when I didn't panic. Besides being present myself, I needed to teach you about empathy, the feelings of others, and how your behaviors affect others. You listened when you were younger.

Later in life, though, I would sometimes start to lecture, and you and your sister would say, "Mom, that's lecture #4,039. We know already!"

I still had to accept that your experiences would become "teachable" moments for you and your sister. I once read that everything we learn about in this world we learn in kindergarten ... but I still don't believe it.

YOUR TURN TO REFLECT

Recall a time when your child showed you they could handle difficulties in their world. They were confident and accepted the world as it was.

_____

_____

_____

_____

_____

How would you describe your child to others?

_____

_____

_____

_____

_____

_____

REFLECTION 5

I LEARN MY CHILD'S LANGUAGE

Dad and I began teaching you to swim in the pool at our apartment complex when you were two years old. We wanted you to never be afraid of the water—mainly because swimming pools were everywhere—and I suspected that you and your sister would eventually like to swim in the ocean when we visited your grandparents in Hawaii.

We enrolled you in swimming classes for toddlers and infants, and you learned to float, splash, and play in the pool by age four. We always kept water wings on your arms, and either Dad or I was always in the water with you. Eventually, you refused the water wings and paddled unassisted for short distances. You loved to swim underwater and play in the pool.

You were five years old when Dad completed his studies at the university, and we had to move out of the married student housing complex. Soon after Dad's graduation, we packed up everything, said our goodbyes to our friends, and left for Dad's new position at a university in another state.

Judging from the change in your behavior after this move, I don't think I did a good job preparing you for this significant change. I think you may have been trying to show us that you were angry with the change, you hated leaving our apartment and the safety of the student housing complex, and you deeply missed your friends.

We moved into an unfurnished rental home in a predominantly white neighborhood where we didn't know anyone. I had taken a job at the university and could no longer be with you at home. We found a babysitter to care for you after school until Dad or I could pick you up. You began first grade in a new school where you knew no one. Often when I was at work, I thought of you and worried you would feel lost and alone. I prayed that you would adjust easily. Despite needing the money and medical benefits from the job, I felt guilty working as a secretary in a doctor's office because I had always been at home with you.

Your first-grade class started to attend swimming lessons weekly at the neighborhood pool. By then, you were a good swimmer, and I thought you'd enjoy the class and feel more comfortable at school. I attended one of the first classes and watched in horror as you just jumped into the pool and swam underwater.

The teacher had been instructing the class about water safety and had specifically said to stay out of the pool until she finished speaking. You, however, swam the entire length of the pool underwater.

The teacher yelled at you to get out.

She scolded you in front of the class, and I felt so bad for you.

I was embarrassed, sad, confused, and angry at what you did, and upset with the teacher for yelling at you in front of the class. Afterward, I talked to her about your skills, but she was still too angry to listen. I scolded you, too, for not listening to her.

Now, I realize I was angry because I was embarrassed by your behavior. I was more concerned about *my* image, because I thought your behavior made me look like a "bad mom" who hadn't taught you to obey adults. I had not been thinking of you … just of myself. I didn't understand that your behavior might still have been a protest of our move and how much you missed your earlier life.

Because Dad and I hadn't understood this, we couldn't comfort you.

We adopted your sister from Korea when you were six. She was almost three years old. She couldn't speak English, so we all struggled to communicate with her.

I only realized afterward that adopting a child—bringing her into our nuclear family—was also a significant change for you. We tried our best to prepare you for your sister, Lee, but when Lee had been with us for only two months, you asked me, "Can we send her back?"

I explained that she was a forever keeper, and I tried to let you and her work out your relationship. After she had been with us for a year, Lee stepped on your favorite record, "Little Red Caboose," and she stomped on the bell of your trumpet.

Somehow you survived.

We also heard the two of you playing with my recorder and giggling together in your room. You recorded, "Twinkle, Twinkle, Little Star," playing off-key on your trumpet and announcing before you started, "This is Grandpa, folks!" You then played the song well and announced into the recorder, "And that was Sean, folks!" We could hear you both laughing gleefully with each other.

Throughout your school years, teachers would call me about your not turning in your homework—and once copying someone else's homework—or distracting other students or not paying attention in class. We received so many calls from the high school that we purchased an answering machine because I hated picking up the phone and listening to a teacher or school administrator rant about your behavior.

I read more parenting and psychology books and tried to figure out whether your behavior was "normal" … or whether it was something beyond the usual teenage angst. I was not sure what to do. What was I missing?

You and your sister were complete enigmas to me. And I was a trained family therapist! I suffered—right along with you—because I didn't know how to help. I hated the phone calls from your schools, and I just wished you both would "behave."

Those school years seemed like a punishment for all of us.

I now wish I had known how to decipher what you were telling me through your behavior. I had been too caught up with making the physical changes needed for our move, and I had downplayed for all of us the emotional transitions of moving to and settling into another state and adopting your sister. I had ignored the feelings of a little boy whose life had been turned on its head.

Now I teach other parents how to listen to their children.

One night when you were in high school, a police officer brought you home, drunk and after curfew. I knew, if that behavior continued, you would soon have a drinking problem, but Dad and I didn't know how to stop it. Instead, and despite our objections, you went to parties at homes where underage drinking was permitted, and you came home drunk.

You no longer listened to us, and we watched in great distress as you self-destructed before our eyes.

I was shocked, but I was also angry that you were embarrassing us and that "everyone" now considered us "bad parents." I was still holding onto you as part of my ego. I now know that was a huge mistake but, in those days, I had not yet begun my journey to sanity and balance.

You threw a rock through a neighbor's window in your senior year. The police charged you with a crime but let it go because your dad said he would help you fix it. You agreed it was wrong to throw the rock, and you repaired the window with Dad. He taught you how to measure, buy, and cut the glass, and insert and anchor it into the window frame. You showed that you had a conscience and a willingness to accept responsibility.

You also learned how to repair windows in the process.

Then you threw a brick through the window of a parked car. We found the owner, paid for the repair, and you worked off your debt with extra chores. A while after that, we saw your nickname spray-painted on a tunnel wall, and we thought you were also connected to that vandalism.

I began to suspect—and fear—that you were displaying your anger all over our neighboring cities. We now knew the police from our town and the bordering towns. The police were lenient, and I was grateful that you were not jailed but "only" placed on probation.

I wondered then if your behavior was somehow related to your coach not playing you in games when you were one of the school team's best baseball players. Or maybe related to the high school teachers and administrators who were accusing you of being racist and forming a White Supremacist Union group on campus. Or maybe to the vice principal who was accusing you of bringing a BB gun on campus and your refusing to tell him it was your friend who had brought it to school.

I worried about you a lot.

Your loyalties, however misplaced, did show me how complex your life was, and the decisions you made showed me you would not be intimidated by authority. You gave me hope, despite my worries about your anger.

Finally, Dad and I gave you a choice to change your school or your friends or to attend counseling. You flatly refused.

What does a parent do when their child refuses to do things the parents' way?

We grounded you for a week. I worried that groundings would continue for months if we didn't do something else. Your sister was also acting out in outrageous ways that Dad and I knew we had to change ... or we would burn out as a family.

When you left for college after high school, your sister missed you immensely, and her behavior, which was already challenging, became worse. Then, like you, she left home in a huff after high school and rarely spoke to us afterward. For a very long time.

Then your dad and I gratefully witnessed the gifts of seeing the two of you work together after you had both left home, seeing you form a deep bond, and helping each other in your adult years.

We finally learned to accept that you and your sister seemed intent on living life in your own ways. We realized we would have to let you do that.

YOUR TURN TO REFLECT

What did you imagine parenting would be like?

_____
_____
_____
_____
_____
_____
_____

What were your dreams?

_____
_____
_____
_____
_____
_____
_____

REFLECTION 6

NURTURING THE SPIRIT OF MY CHILDREN—IT WILL GET THEM THROUGH LIFE

Sean, I suspect that you were always independent. God made you that way and you live it. You see the world with wonder, and you see problems as puzzles to solve. People are attracted to you because you possess a strong, infectious, charismatic resilience and an infectious determination to live life fully.

You have a history of people liking your spirit. Your first-grade teacher confided in me that she thought you were gifted. She saw you as a bright child and picked you to help other children in the class.

Your second-grade teacher, however, approached me about several rubber erasers you might have stolen from the class, but she could not prove it. I was upset with the accusation and wondered what I had done wrong for you to steal objects from school. I looked through your room but found nothing. Fifteen years later, I found four rubber erasers and made the connection. I realized that we had moved from one state to another between grade one and grade two, so you were then in an unfamiliar town, a school with new children, new adults in your life, and your sister, Lee, had just arrived from Korea. She was almost three years old, could not speak English, cried a lot, and demanded my attention. I now worked out of the home and could not be with you as I used to be.

I use the erasers today to remind me how a young child might try to cope with being ripped away from a wonderfully familiar world and then be forced to adapt to a new alien one … now with a sister in it.

Your fourth- and fifth-grade teacher told me how you would fail if you didn't turn in your homework. When you did do your homework, you refused to turn it in. Then, after you turned in an assignment, she accused you of copying your friend's homework. And after scolding you, you admitted that you had. She always complained to me about you, but in her strictness, she was fair. You respected her. You also stood up for your classmates when you felt they were unfairly treated by others. Despite many complaints about your behavior from your teacher, she passed you both years. In thinking back, your refusal to comply may have been your way of telling us that you hated change. Indeed, when you left home and asked for the living room rugs and furniture and other items from our home to furnish your home, we gave them to you. I realize that these may have been transitional objects, familiar objects to remind you of home, to help ease the pain of change.

Dad and I were relieved when you managed to pass out of middle school without too many incidents. That reprieve was short-lived, though, as the high school principal constantly complained to us about you.

Your ninth-grade algebra teacher often sat you in the hallway during class because of incidents in the classroom that he partly blamed on you. He asked me to talk to you about disrupting the class, but he neglected to tell me he made you sit in the hallway most days.

You said you could handle the situation, so I never got involved with that teacher. I wondered how you would complete his course, but I just crossed my fingers and prayed. Somehow you passed Algebra I, but I decided I had had enough when you took Algebra II with the same teacher the following year. I told you that you had to get through the class because I did not want to deal with your teacher anymore.

It was still all about me.

Over the Christmas holidays and for much of the following January, Dad and I began panicking that you would not be able to pass Algebra II. I tutored you forcefully ... even when you protested. We spent hours reviewing and memorizing formulas, and you showed me how answers were derived and explained all the different procedures for doing that. I wrote algebraic equations on sticky notes, pasted them to the bathroom mirror, and quizzed you relentlessly. We were exhausted after a few weeks, but you seemed to be in a better position to pass the course.

You did pass the course at the end of the year, and we all celebrated with relief.

I worried you would struggle in your next math class, so I insisted you attend summer school to review Algebra II. I thought a summer review course would reinforce the concepts you had learned and prepare you for the next year. Selfishly, I also didn't want to hear from any more teachers.

"It's a waste of time," you said, and we began our arguing over summer school.

"My tutoring may not have wholly prepared you for the next math class," I pleaded.

Finally, reluctantly, you agreed to attend summer school.

When you came home that summer after the second class, you slammed the front door and threw your book on the kitchen table.

"I told you so!" you yelled at me. "I had to correct the teacher when he worked through a problem on the board! I'm not going back!"

I thought to myself, *This kid knows himself better than I do.*

Even so, I yelled back at you. "Yes, you are going back. You will learn more by correcting the teacher!"

It was a pleasant day for both of us when you finished summer school with an A.

I decided then to try to listen, observe, learn, and set aside my assumptions about my children. I saw you tutoring others and gaining self-confidence during summer school. Perhaps your reason for going was not really to learn something new but to gain self-confidence and know you might have something to offer this world.

YOUR TURN TO REFLECT

How did your child express their true nature?

_____
_____
_____
_____
_____
_____
_____

Identify one way you have nurtured and one way you have hindered its expression.

_____
_____
_____
_____
_____
_____
_____

REFLECTION 7

CHILDREN DISCOVER THEMSELVES IN MANY WAYS

Sean, you and your sister did not have Asian role models as teachers, coaches, pastors, and communities, as I had had. This fact first hit me when you came home in the ninth grade, threw yourself on your bed, and yelled, "It's all your fault!"

Confused, I stood in the doorway and asked, "What did I do? What are you talking about?"

Sobbing, you replied, "It's because of you I have all this hair!"

I understood. I am Okinawan, and we are known for our hairy bodies. You were beginning puberty and were growing body hair, where most white boys were not. You had thick, bushy eyebrows and hair on your arms, legs, back, and chest whereas white boys had little or none. You had a full head of strong, wavy black hair that did not bend easily, so you kept your head shaved.

My heart melted for you. I knew the boys at your school were growing up at different rates and would compare their bodies to each other's. Being an Asian of Okinawan descent, you would be growing hair all over your body. You would look like no one else, not even other Japanese of non-Okinawan descent. Even your dad, whose family came from Hiroshima, Japan, did not have the hair you had.

These purely physical differences, which neither you nor I could control and which upset you, made me sad. I knew how important it was for you—for any teenager—to be like others. We took you to Hawaii often to let you see your Okinawan cousins and uncles, the large Asian population that looked like you, and to know you were okay just the way you were.

I remember your telling us how you, your cousin, and his friends purchased a trunk full of illegal fireworks for a New Year's celebration, and how you sweated nervously while driving home with them, wondering what would happen if the car got into an accident and blew up. You loved your cousins' free spirits and thinking. They looked like you and you could identify with them. Your family in Hawaii welcomed and embraced you, and I saw you relax and be your playful self whenever we were in Hawaii.

Once when you played on the community American Legion baseball team and were selected to be part of our city's traveling team, you came home from a game and described an upsetting incident. But from this story, I learned you had a quick wit and sense of humor. Your team had been playing in a rural town in the neighboring state. A few of the players from the other team, all white, approached you and your African-American friends.

"Can we smell you?" they asked.

"Why?" you asked, startled.

"We haven't seen people like you guys," they explained, "and we were told that you smell different from us. Can we smell you?"

"Sure, if we can smell you guys too!" you laughingly retorted.

YOUR TURN TO REFLECT

When and how did your child notice that they were different from others?

What was their experience like for you?

REFLECTION 8

LETTING GO

As you and your sister grew up, I learned a difficult lesson: we never could control your behavior. When we suggested that you change schools and friends, you refused. When we offered counseling, you declined.

What does a parent do when their child refuses to do things "your way" and only does them "their way"?

When you were fifteen, you asked if you could build a skateboard ramp in the backyard. We considered the ramp's liability, its cost, and the plans we'd need before agreeing to your request. We wanted to prepare you for the world by building your self-confidence and resilience to disappointment, criticism, and challenges in life and we thought that building the ramp might do that.

We knew you were smart, but we saw your true brilliance for the first time. You methodically designed the ramp with your protractor, ruler, and other tools; calculated the lumber, nails, and joints needed for the project; researched the cost; and listed the tools and labor you'd need to build the ramp. As we watched you build the ramp, a determined teenager, it was like watching your two-year-old self again, playing with his Lego sets, concentrating, and using his imagination.

You organized your friends to help, and their parents eagerly donated money for the lumber and nails. They lent saws, hammers, and whatever else was needed to complete the project. Your friends happily labored under your direction after their parents had signed liability waivers. In a month, the ramp was up and ready to go.

It was beautiful and fitted perfectly into the space of our small backyard. Everyone was happy and excited, and it remained pure heaven for a few months. At one neighbor's suggestion, you and your friends hung a net around the ramp so the skateboards wouldn't fly into his backyard.

Then came the downsides. We learned that one boy had broken his ankle on the ramp. Then we found some boys smoking marijuana in the back of the ramp, and finally we discovered empty beer bottles and dog poop in the backyard.

We decided to shut down the ramp and asked you to dismantle it.

You didn't protest, and I wondered whether you were actually as relieved as we were. You and your friends dismantled the ramp without incident and removed all the debris in the yard.

We were proud that you accepted the responsibility for the ramp; it reassured us that you were growing up.

We learned we needed to give you experiences for you to grow in your own way. I knew that you liked to figure out challenges, and you had by then shown a remarkable ability to turn within yourself for answers and use your imagination for solutions.

I would like to think that, without even knowing we were doing it, we nurtured your soul and your intuition to grow and express yourself in the world.

I knew I had to let you go when you left for college. I could no longer protect you as I had done when you were at home.

Always with Much Love and Deep Aloha,
Mom

YOUR TURN TO REFLECT

What challenges did you face when you allowed your child to do what they wanted to do, realizing it might be dangerous?

_____

_____

_____

_____

_____

_____

How did you make the decision?

_____

_____

_____

_____

_____

_____

PART TWO

A LETTER TO MY DAUGHTER

Those who flow as life flows know they need no other force.

Lao Tzu

My Dearest Lee,

Dad, your brother, and I waited nervously behind a glass wall at the international terminal with a group of other families. I think everyone there was waiting for "the kids from Korea." We peered intently at all the children deplaning with adult escorts and we tried to recognize and find you.

We kept glancing at the photo we had of you and scrutinized all the children's faces, but we didn't see you. My stomach was knotted with anxiety, and I worried that you might have missed the flight. Then, from back in the cabin of the plane, we heard loud wails and sobbing.

We figured that must be you.

The social worker who introduced us to you warned that you hated being awakened from a nap or a deep sleep, and would always cry with anger and irritation. I knew then that you were already showing your strong will. I wondered what lay ahead for us as a family.

You were almost three years old that day when you emerged next to us in the airport. You were wearing a bright red jacket with tiny white flowers and tiny blue slip-on sneakers with cartoon characters on them. Your chaperone held your hand and tried to comfort you as she escorted you through immigration. We followed on the other side of the glass wall, fascinated that you would soon be part of our family. Your brother looked at you and said nothing.

Once you cleared immigration, your escort brought you to us, introduced you, and passed your hand over to mine. She explained that we were *Umma* (Korean for "mom") and *Appa* (Korean for "dad").

Then she smiled and left.

My fear and anxiety quickly and surprisingly turned to excitement, and my heart knew that we were up to the task of embracing, protecting, and loving you. You looked so tiny, so confused, and so vulnerable. You were probably wondering, *What am I doing here?* and *Who are these people?*

Dad and I looked at each other and your brother scrutinized you, still without a word.

Then I did panic. *What have we done? Who are you? Will you like us? Can we bond and be a family?*

Little did I know then that you would teach me that unconditional love is born in conflict, arguments, disciplining, crying, yelling, screaming, and distrust of each other, but it still grows, without conscious effort, in the process of becoming a family.

YOUR TURN TO REFLECT

What changed in your family when a second child arrived?

---- REFLECTION 9 ----

NEVER ASSUME WHAT IS FALSE TO BE TRUE

We wanted you and Sean to have broad life experiences and to face challenges under our guidance. To teach you about your family, we flew to Hawaii and showed you the islands. We fished, camped—once, at least—and drove to Seattle to visit your grandma, grandpa, and auntie.

When your brother was eight years old and you were five, we tried cross-country skiing in the nearby mountains. None of us had skied before, so we had to learn together from an instructor. It was difficult, but we skied cross-country and enjoyed the challenge. We slept together in a cabin with several beds, but you began to snore so loudly that no one could sleep. Dad and I made a bed of blankets in the bathtub and placed you in it, with more blankets over you to stay warm, just so we could get some sleep.

We had thought we were being clever, putting you in the bathtub, and we thought we would have a private joke and a fun memory for our family. However, I had second thoughts the next day. Because you had only been with us for a little over two years, I wondered whether you understood our humor or if you would mistake that bathtub incident as rejection. I didn't know.

Raising you was so different from raising your brother. I had read and was cautioned by the social worker that we should expect difficulty understanding each other after adoption and that we would have to adjust to each other. For example, you arrived with little blue slip-on tennis shoes. We had purchased tie-on tennis shoes for you and expected to teach you how to lace them. After many trials, you learned and we all were proud of your achievement. Then you decided not to tie your shoes and walked dragging your laces around on the ground. We kept telling you to tie your laces but had to wait for you to trip over them for you to decide to tie them consistently. We were all right-handed whereas you were left-handed. It took me a while, but I learned to place your water cup on your left side since you kept knocking it over when I put it on the right, as I would for the rest of us. I also knew you might have to deal with the trauma of leaving your home for another land, so I tried to develop patience with your many crying tantrums.

I tried my best to be a good mother but I never knew if I was successful.

Shortly after you arrived, I wanted to show you our neighborhood. You held my hand, and we walked on the sidewalk for me to show you the houses, the park, the cars, and the street. I pointed at and named everything to teach you English.

One day you suddenly ran ahead of me on one of our walks. You tripped on a sidewalk broken up by a large tree root and fell flat on your face. The fall scratched your nose and head, but I saw that you weren't severely hurt. I wondered why you hadn't held your hands out to catch yourself. After that, Dad and I took you to the park to help you develop motor skills, because we weren't sure how well you could run or kick a ball, or whether you knew how to play in the sand. We showed you the sandbox, the jungle gym, and a children's slide to see if you knew what to do.

You circled far away from the slide but slowly approached the sandbox as if you were not sure what it was for. I showed you how to dig in the sand and how to make sand mountains we could smash. You liked that, and you played with me for a bit. Then Dad and I took you to the children's slide. You didn't want to mount it, but you watched what the other children did. Then you walked back and watched the other children playing in the sand, running and catching each other and laughing together, but you kept returning to the slide.

I thought you might want to slide down like the other children, so I took your hand and helped you climb to the top of the slide. You hesitated and then you cried when I said it was okay to go down the slide. We changed tactics. Dad waited at the bottom to catch us while you and I slid down the slide together. The first time down, you clung to me but didn't cry. Then you wanted to do it again. So we did it again and Dad caught us again at the bottom. After several times sliding down together, you did it by yourself.

Our hunch was that you had not had much physical activity in Korea and you needed to develop your eye-hand coordination and balance. Without considering the emotional trauma from the adoption, we focused on physical exercise, thinking that gaining confidence in your body would help you build your self-confidence. You were always timid about physical activity, but I enrolled you in ballet classes, hoping that with the help of a teacher you would become more comfortable with your body. That plan lasted about two months until you fell on your face while crossing the street. You pulled me down with you as I was holding your hand, and after that, you refused to return to the ballet classes. Eventually, you took up gymnastics at the YWCA, loved it, did cartwheels, and talked of going to the Olympics, which made us happy.

Next, we enrolled you in swimming classes. You swam for a few years, becoming quite good on the swim team and winning competitions. We kept hoping that you would keep building your self-confidence by developing your muscles and eye-hand coordination.

Many years later, only after you had become an adult, I learned that a predictable environment helps a person who has been traumatized function better. I hadn't realized that we may have prolonged your trauma by introducing you to new things and new environments too soon, thinking then that those new challenges would help you gain confidence.

Books on parenting suggest that different experiences would help build self-confidence, but what if our good intentions re-traumatized you because what we had read did not apply to you?

You and your brother taught me that even acting from my best intentions could be harmful.

YOUR TURN TO REFLECT

Describe a challenging moment while raising your second or third child.

Did you parent your second or third child differently from your firstborn?

―――― REFLECTION 10 ――――

I LEARNED PATIENCE OVER THE YEARS IN BONDING WITH MY CHILD

You developed a strong relationship with another girl while in the sixth grade. She lived with her divorced mother and they invited you to spend time at their home after school. I started becoming concerned, because you were spending most of your time there, rather than at our home, and we were still trying to build a relationship with you.
    One day you called me at work.
    "May I please speak with Mrs. Yabusaki," you said.
    "Yes," I said, annoyed. I knew you recognized my voice. "This is your mother!"
    "Mrs. Yabusaki," you replied, "can I sleep at my friend's house tonight?"
    I was furious. *Why would you not acknowledge me as "mom"? Why did your friend's mom always allow you to spend the night there? You have spent too many nights there already,* I thought.

"No! Come home," I told you.

You refused.

I felt like you were running away from home and that your friend's mom was interfering with our attempts to bond with you. When I returned home from work, though, you were in your room, pouting.

I realized that our personalities and temperaments were different, and I wasn't sure how—or if—you and I could bond. I wondered if we would create one loving family with you more quickly than we were doing, but it was clear that you had a mind of your own … even about "bonding."

In your eighth grade, a neighbor caught you and your best friend, who also happened to be adopted, emptying other people's mailboxes and throwing their mail into the street. I was called by a police officer that afternoon, and after I had spoken with him, they placed you on juvenile probation.

I was furious. Again. I had never ever been stopped or apprehended by the police in my life, and now we were known to police departments in three counties, thanks to the antics of you and your brother.

Next, you began cutting classes and smoking marijuana routinely while you were still only in the eighth grade and on probation. Dad and I were never able to find you after the school day, because you hid from us so well.

I never knew why, but one day you came home immediately after school and called me at work to confirm you were home. I don't know why you listened to us at that point, but you complied. Your dad and I were relieved.

You still had more surprises for us, however.

The vice principal called us one day for a student-parent-teacher conference to discuss your situation at school. At the meeting, they warned me that you might fail eighth grade because you were failing most of your subjects. You weren't doing your homework or handing it in and you were cutting classes. I couldn't help but wonder whether you were stoned in class too.

I nodded to the teacher and the vice principal. I understood that they wanted your dad and me to do something, but I didn't know what else we could do to curb your behavior. Frankly, we simply felt you were ignoring us. While I spoke with the teachers, you sat there silently.

The vice principal told me the school was considering holding you back a year.

"Her redoing eighth grade would be fine with us," I said. "The consequences of repeating a year might teach her more about responsibility than we can."

Your homeroom teacher sympathized with you, however. He objected to this plan and adamantly told all of us in the room that you deserved to pass eighth grade. He thought you were smart, and he said you should move on to the ninth grade. He even offered to tutor you after school to help you raise your grades.

I was surprised but so happy to hear that he was that invested in your success.

"Thank you," I said. "I'm very grateful. But it's okay for her to fail, too."

In truth, I was addressing you, at that point, not him. I wanted you to hear my willingness to let you fail. I wanted you to hear that so you had the chance to assume responsibility for your choices. If you were going to fight with me over this, I decided I would not engage in the fight, and I forced myself to disengage my investment in your passing. I hoped you would learn that if you failed, you would be hurting yourself, not me.

I finally realized I had to step aside and let go of wanting something for you more than it seemed you wanted that something for yourself. I saw that by imposing my will I had impeded you from finding out about life your own way. Whether you passed or failed was of no concern to me. By now, I had learned to let go of other people's judgment of me, so I no longer thought of myself as a bad mother by allowing you to fail eighth grade. We would deal with the consequences afterward. More important to your dad and me was that you would learn to take responsibility for your own decisions and actions, and know we would always be there for you.

We would continue to monitor your safety and be present for you, but the decision to pass or fail eighth grade had to be yours. Perhaps failing a grade could be a teachable moment for you, we decided. We knew you prided yourself on being a good student, and we gambled that you would pull yourself together enough to pass.

With the help of your teacher, you completed eighth grade and went on to high school.

YOUR TURN TO REFLECT

What did you learn about yourself as your children grew?

_____

_____

_____

_____

_____

What are your three best traits as a parent?

_____

_____

_____

_____

_____

_____

REFLECTION 11

PICKING MY BATTLES TO WIN THE WAR

Your teenage years tried my soul, just as your brother's had. In ninth grade, you began wearing tight-fitting, short skirts that barely covered your butt, and shirts that revealed too much of your belly and breasts. Despite my objections, you snuck out of the house to apply black eyeliner, mascara, pink rouge, and bright red lipstick before school, and I only found that out because you came home one day wearing makeup. I suspected you had purchased the makeup or had gotten samples from the department store or that your friends shared theirs with you.

Your brother complained to me one day that his friends thought you looked like a "Ho" (a whore), and he told me that guys were grabbing your ass as you walked up the stairwell at school. He was embarrassed and he wanted you to stop wearing such revealing clothes.

After several months of what I called "nonsense dressing," I stormed into your bedroom one afternoon with a trash bag and began sorting through all the clothes in your closet and drawers. I had had enough of your dressing like a "Ho," and my unsuccessful demands that you wear proper clothing. I threw all your short skirts and tight-fitting, midriff-revealing tops into a bag and left you with only a pair of jeans and a few hip-length t-shirts. I felt like a prison warden, but I didn't know what else to do.

To my surprise, with the money you had earned at your job as a server at the local ice cream store, you then bought new clothes that were tasteful and appropriate. We never discussed that incident, but you did give me "stink eyes" for weeks afterward, although you never again questioned my rules for appropriate dress.

Our next battle was over makeup. Despite my continuing objections, I caught you wearing heavy black eyeliner, bright red lipstick, and rouge when I wasn't around. I was tired of arguing though, and didn't say much. I decided I would pick other battles to win the war.

When you came home with pink eye from sampling makeup at the department store, you asked us for help.

Dad told me he relished the opportunity to scare you about infections. In his most graphic and dramatic yet scientific way, he explained the risks of using other people's makeup and described how diseases spread. We quietly smiled and thanked the universe for allowing us to teach you about safety and an opportunity to help you as we took you to the doctor for treatment. We never spoke about makeup again, and you never used anyone else's makeup or got another infection.

When you were in the tenth grade, Dad and I found a used condom in the garbage can in your bedroom. I had thought you would not have sex until you were married. I was so naïve.

When we confronted you about having sex in our house, you called me a "bitch" and stormed off to your room. I chased after you and when I caught up with you, I grabbed you with both hands, pushed you onto your back on the bed, and then straddled myself over you. I raised my hand, about to slap you when suddenly, a thought popped into my mind that stopped me. *What am I doing? She is my daughter! This is child abuse!*

I could not hit you because I realized, right then and there, how much I loved you.

I bent down close to your ear as I straddled you and whispered angrily, "You'll never get rid of me!"

"I am inside you!" I hissed.

I jumped off you, startled that I had said that, but I knew deep down that I had bonded with you through unconditional love. I knew nothing could break that bond. You could not get rid of me even if you tried.

I left your room a bit confused but no longer angry. It had taken twelve years for me to understand that I loved you deeply, unconditionally, despite all the difficulties we had shared. I knew for certain that you were our daughter, no matter what challenges we had had or what challenges might still lie ahead.

During your eleventh-grade year, Lee, I was working as a clerk for a doctor while going to school for my degree in family therapy. I returned early from work one day to find two police officers talking to you and a boy in a car in front of the house. Alarmed, I asked the officers what the problem was. They said they had a call from one of our neighbors that you and your boyfriend were smoking marijuana in the car.

You both denied smoking, and I confirmed that you weren't under the influence by sniffing your clothes and car for the smell of marijuana. When I told the police that I was your mother and was willing to take responsibility for you, they left.

That was the first time I had met or even known about your boyfriend, and I saw that he was African-American. You were parked in a white neighborhood, and I thought the neighbors might have been alarmed that an African-American boy was "loitering" in the area. I was upset with the neighbors for possibly being afraid of this boy, with you for hanging out in a car alone with him, and with him for not being aware of the neighborhood and potentially putting you both at risk.

Most of all, you and I argued about what you were doing alone with any boy in a car.

I realized, as I had with your brother, that I couldn't protect you from harm. I decided that when you were ready to listen, I would teach you about racism. Meanwhile, you would have to wrestle with the issues of racism and sort out your identity as a Korean child adopted into a Japanese-American family.

By this time, I had a degree in family therapy and had opened a private practice to help families navigate their challenges in life. I was also in a doctoral degree program in psychology trying to finish my dissertation. I went to school believing that all the knowledge I gained would make me a better parent and advisor to other families. And I enjoyed learning. But I could not concentrate on my clients, school, or even on our family because of all the chaos in our lives. I finally admitted that I was too distracted by all that was happening with you and Sean and all the drama in our family. Something would have to go.

I canceled all my family therapy clients and consulting appointments, put my dissertation on hold, and withdrew from community volunteer responsibilities. I closed my practice, too embarrassed to advertise myself as a family therapist when our family was in such chaos. Clearly I needed to know more about parenting, and I focused on you three. I realized that both of you and Dad were more important to me than anything else in life.

Since conventional psychological and family therapy theories and research were not working for me, I decided to search for answers on parenting from a spiritual perspective. I needed help from a higher realm, but I wasn't sure how to get it.

I started reading books on spirituality, meditation, Taoism, Confucianism, Zen Buddhism, and other philosophies. I read the *Tao Te Ching* (translates roughly as "the way of integrity"). I meditated on Zen *koans* and used those riddles—puzzles—to demonstrate to myself the limitation of the logical mind and to gain greater truth through further intuitive insight. I started accessing and using my own intuition, and I became more confident in my spiritual aspect.

I enjoyed yoga, attended meditation retreats and workshops, spent moments alone every day to read and meditate, and exercised regularly to reduce stress.

My fears and doubts began to dissipate.

What I had seen as problems with you and Sean became lessons for myself, reflections. Lao Tzu's saying, "When the student is ready, the teacher will appear," meant something new. You children were my teachers—I just hadn't known it. My stubbornness to be "right" had needed the strong antidote of your presence for me to confront—and change—my perfectionism.

YOUR TURN TO REFLECT

Recall a memorable event with your children that forced you to grow. What did you learn?

REFLECTION 12

LETTING GO IS AN ART, NOT A SCIENCE, SO I'M TRUSTING MY GUT

I was finally learning the powerful lesson of letting go of my children while still keeping them close.

I knew I wanted to keep you safe, but I always wondered when to allow you to be on your own. I realized that maybe it wasn't just my decision when it was time to let you go. You would leave when you wanted to, not when I decided it was time.

I grappled with what were the appropriate limits to set for our children. Did I trust you to make healthy decisions for your lives?

If you were to follow your *tao*—your own path—I had to be the one to change. I had to be the one to respect and accept your wishes.

I was still feeling my way through parenting.

At about that time, we found large holes in your bedroom window screen, and we figured you were sneaking out through them at night to visit your boyfriend. We had told you it was okay to see your boyfriend at his home—which may have been safer than ours because he lived in a diverse neighborhood and his parents worried about his safety from racism, too. We told you that you needed to be home by midnight; that was your curfew.

Instead, you continued to sneak in and out after curfew, even after Dad and I had lectured, scolded, and grounded you. We finally forbade you to visit your boyfriend if you couldn't return home by midnight.

You still snuck out.

Finally, one morning I stormed up to you in the kitchen and, trying to control my anger, I grabbed you by the shoulder and turned you around to face me.

"We are locking up the house at curfew," I said. "You won't be able to get in if you aren't home by then. If you choose to come home after that, you will have to find somewhere else to sleep."

When you returned home the next night at two a.m., two hours after your curfew, Dad and I lay in bed and listened to your trying to get in. You didn't have the key to the deadbolt and rang the doorbell, but we stayed in bed. We had also locked your window, suspecting that you would try to sneak in that way. We heard you try, and when there were no more sounds, we thought you must have given up and left.

We assumed you'd gone to your boyfriend's family for the night as that family never turned you away, but we never knew for sure. The following morning, you returned and said nothing. Neither did we.

You were never out past curfew again.

I felt as though I had given you and your brother over ten thousand lectures by then. Just as your brother had, you began telling me, "Mom, that was lecture #2,053!"

I knew by then, Lee, that simply talking with you didn't work. We needed to act, but I was always afraid we might endanger you by setting such firm limits, even though it seemed right to put you in control of your choices. So, we told you to come home on time or be locked out. You could take school seriously or fail a grade. You could dress appropriately or I would throw away your clothes.

I started to learn to trust my gut and to accept that I could not control every outcome of your actions. I could, however, try to make it as safe as possible for you to learn from your choices.

I decided it was okay for me to be bold.

YOUR TURN TO REFLECT

Do any of the stories remind you of challenges raising your children or your working with children?

_____

_____

_____

_____

_____

_____

How did you decide what to do when challenged as a parent or caregiver?

_____

_____

_____

_____

_____

_____

_____

REFLECTION 13

THERE IS NO SUCH THING AS TAKING A BREAK FROM PARENTING

Dad and I felt as though we needed a little break from you and your brother, but we weren't sure whether we could trust you and him to be okay on your own. Still, we wanted a date night … and we wanted to trust you.

So one afternoon we left home at about five p.m., but I had forgotten something and we returned at about seven. As we neared the house, we saw that all the house lights were on, and we heard loud music pulsating throughout the neighborhood. When we entered the front door, Sean and his friends scrambled to hide their beers and look casual.

We were furious, and we threw everyone out. We told Sean he was grounded, and you retreated to your room.

When you were both a little older, we left again for an overnight trip and hoped we could trust you to stay safe. When we returned, I found another condom in your bedroom trash can.

I was furious.

We confronted you with what we had found, although I knew nothing would stop you from having sex. I was secretly glad you had at least used a condom ... and possibly other birth control methods. We learned then that you were already taking the pill. I should have trusted that you would have found Planned Parenthood and protected yourself. That showed how little I knew you.

I wondered, though, *How did you know about Planned Parenthood? Who told you?* We never talked about sex because you weren't talking to us in general and you flat-out refused to talk about sex.

Several months after that incident, you approached Dad about having contracted a vaginal infection. You had gone to Planned Parenthood to check yourself out and discovered you had a possible sexually transmitted disease (STD). It seemed this was your first experience with an STD, and you were scared. I was glad you had had the common sense to check it out and grateful that you trusted Dad enough to ask for his help.

I overheard the conversation from the kitchen while I was cooking dinner. I knew you could approach Dad more easily than me, so I stayed out of your heart-to-heart talk with him—one of the few you two had—so as not to spoil it.

Dad, always waiting for an opportunity to teach you safety, immediately embellished the horrible details of an STD.

"Eew!" I heard him say. I knew he was probably wrinkling his nose. "That's *Condyloma acuminata*. If you're not careful, it can spread and affect your ability to have children. Here's what happens ..." Even if it wasn't *Condyloma acuminata*, Dad wanted to make your anogenital warts sound awful. They were!

He continued reciting all the gruesome details about everything an infection can do to your body and confirmed the treatment you were receiving. We silently thanked the universe for your allowing us to help you monitor the situation.

Later, Dad and I chuckled when you told your boyfriend you thought you had got it from him. And then your boyfriend accused you of giving it to him.

YOUR TURN TO REFLECT

How did you adapt to your child's or children's growing independence and sexuality?

What values and beliefs of yours did their independence challenge?

REFLECTION 14

SOMETIMES, THE BEST WAY TO TEACH IS THROUGH "NATURAL CONSEQUENCES"

We decided to use "natural consequences" to teach you responsibility because our lectures, groundings, withheld privileges, increased household chores, and other parenting suggestions were not working. We decided it was time to allow your environment to teach you.

In the tenth grade, you asked for a private phone line in the house. We told you we couldn't afford one, but we offered to pay for its installation if you paid the monthly bills. You found a job at the nearby ice cream shop almost immediately.

From what you told us, you did a great job serving customers … while killing the cockroaches that ran across the counters. You showed us how you would slam the service counter, scatter the bugs that had hidden under the napkin containers, and then spray them as they came out, all before the customers arrived.

After about eight months, you quit that job. You couldn't pay your phone bill without that income, and the phone company canceled your line. You quickly found another job, paid to reinstall the line, and never missed a payment again.

Dad and I were surprised and elated that you never argued or blamed us for losing your phone line. We were amazed at your determination to keep that phone line, and we were so grateful that we got through that situation without fights. You learned never to quit a job again without first having a new one to go to.

In your high school years, we bought our first answering machine because the schools were calling us so often. I refused to pick up the telephone for those calls anymore, but one day I inadvertently picked up the phone. Without saying hello or introducing herself, a teacher yelled at me. I had met her before and recognized her voice.

"Your daughter is always late for school!" she shouted in my ear. "Where do you live, anyway?"

"We live across the street from the school," I answered calmly. I was so fed up with all the calls by then that I no longer reacted to them.

She hung up on me.

I decided you needed to be accountable to your teachers and the school, even if you refused to be accountable to me. I would no longer excuse or minimize your behavior to the school authorities or rescue you from them. As in your eighth grade year, I refused to give any more excuses for you.

Finally, in your eleventh grade, you had begun doing your homework at your desk at home. Dad and I were thrilled, although we weren't sure what you were learning. We only had until the next school year before you left home, and we wanted to be sure that you could—and would—think through situations and not be governed purely by your feelings.

But how to do that?

YOUR TURN TO REFLECT

What was the most challenging moment for you when raising your children?

Were you surprised with your response? Why? Or why not?

REFLECTION 15

THE MEDIATED LEARNING EXPERIENCE SAVED MY SANITY

As you had spiraled "out of control" and challenged us so much in high school, I decided to try something completely different.

I took a course on alternative ways of understanding intelligence quotient (IQ) and other psychological assessments on cognition. A special education teacher who had become my mentor and friend taught us about a method to encourage children to learn how to learn and challenge the connection between IQ and learning. We saw that *learning to learn* was far more important than having a high IQ score. I was inspired when I learned we could teach these learning skills.

I did my doctoral research on children's learning styles and Mediated Learning with one hundred fifth-grade children in public schools. Dad and I were so impressed with my results that we decided to apply the method to you.

If we couldn't "talk sense" into you, we would create experiences that would teach you how to think. Thinking skills would be our gift to you.

What I had learned was designed for classroom and academic use, but I thought we might be able to use the same principles in broader areas of your life.

In Mediated Learning, a teacher or parent essentially engages in open-ended communication with a child about the "how" and the "why" of any subject being studied, not necessarily about the "what" of the topic itself. By encouraging the child to consider these broader aspects of the subject—or of a problem—a more complete understanding can be achieved.

Sometimes the force used in a classroom or at home to "push" a student into new material can create resistance in the student. The method I learned tries to avoid this involuntary resistance.

I think Lao Tzu would have loved this philosophy of teaching. I interpret Lao Tzu's teaching in this situation as implying that when we insist a child should learn in a way that is contrary to their nature, we create resistance; they resist the learning. It can be fruitless. There is no way of deviating from a child's natural way of learning or knowing and it may be better to try another way that is congruent with the child's nature.

Before your senior year in high school, school had seemed unimportant to you. Ever since the eighth grade, you had been on the verge of failing or getting Ds in some of your classes, and we wondered whether you would even graduate from high school. You had ignored curfew, snuck out of the house late at night, returned early the following day, and were consistently late for school. You broke almost all our family rules without remorse. It seemed as though we had grounded you for most of your life, but nothing had changed your rebellious behavior.

Dad and I decided to apply Mediated Learning principles and teach you to think critically by asking you questions and, thereby, indirectly, teaching you how to learn. The theory suggests that both learning and thinking can become rewarding in themselves when there is no resistance, and people who think better, of course, adapt better to life. In contrast, the theory suggested that traditional education relied too heavily on memorizing answers and was far too passive, albeit forceful, an experience.

Nothing else had worked on you, so we decided to give this theory a try. We asked ourselves, "Could critical thinking really change Lee's behavior?"

Dad started with our first test. One evening during dinner, he casually asked you, "So, what are you learning in anthropology class?"

With your usual scowl, you looked up and answered, "We're watching a video."

"Why are you watching a video?" Dad followed up. "Anything, in particular, you're supposed to learn?"

You sighed and rolled your eyeballs as if these were stupid questions.

"I don't know ..." you replied, exasperated. "For entertainment?"

I sat there silently, outraged at your attitude.

Nonplussed, Dad continued.

"Why not ask the teacher what you're supposed to be learning and why? Otherwise, it seems like a huge waste of time."

He then changed the subject. He and I knew that if he said too much, he would end up lecturing you, and the two of you would be in an argument with no resolution. The point was to stay civil and keep engaging you in conversation.

When you came home from school the next day, you walked up to your father when he returned from work.

"Well, my teacher said I should know," you announced.

Dad was surprised you had even asked your teacher.

"Really?" he asked. "Do you?"

"No," you said, stomping to your room and slamming the door.

"Well," Dad yelled after you, "we're going to ask your teacher at the back-to-school night! You need to know why you're watching the video."

I could tell he was upset.

"Sure! Whatever!" you shouted at him through your bedroom door.

On the back-to-school night, which was designed to show parents what their children were doing in class, I decided to see your anthropology class teacher by myself. I didn't want to risk overwhelming your teacher with two upset parents.

I introduced myself and asked her the purpose of viewing the video you had mentioned to Dad.

"My daughter didn't know why she was watching it," I said innocently, hoping the other parents would also be interested in the answer. I felt comfortable asking her because I really wanted to know too.

Your teacher looked surprised and laughed.

"Your daughter should know what the video is about. She's one of my best students. You know she's getting an A in the class, don't you?"

I was surprised and told her what you told us: "Lee thought it was for entertainment."

Her smile faded quickly, and she glared at me. I wondered why was she glaring at me.

Instead, she paused for a second and spoke calmly. "We're studying stories from different cultures about the origins of humankind."

"Wow," I said. "Interesting stuff. I'll be sure to let Lee know what she's supposed to learn from the video. Thank you!"

I felt I now knew that we had to help you create meaning for this task so you could view the video with purpose. Later that evening, I recounted the meeting with your teacher to Dad and you. Dad stayed silent. We were both more interested in your response.

"Really?" you quietly responded. "Hmm."

That was all you said.

We were shocked, but we were cautiously excited because you had listened quietly and responded without rolling your eyeballs or yelling or swearing at us.

Was this a result of our sincere interest in your learning, we wondered.

The next day after you came home from school, you rushed into the kitchen looking for me. I could tell you were angry.

"Do you know what my teacher said about you?" you asked me. "She told me that you tried to embarrass *me* last night ... in front of the other parents!"

"Well," I asked, "Who do *you* think should be embarrassed?"

You paused a second, thrown off guard. You thought for a minute.

"My teacher," you said, "for not telling us what we were supposed to learn from that video."

"Yep," I said. "If you know what you're supposed to be learning and why, then you'll pay attention and probably know what might be on your teacher's next test. Good for you!"

I even high-fived you then, Lee. Remember?

Then I turned to hide my smile and, mentally pumping my fists, thought, *Yes! My daughter is learning!*

For the next year, Dad and I continued to ask you questions—rather than give you advice—about everything. We probed your reasoning, we made observations, and we questioned your assumptions, but only for as long as you stayed interested in our conversation. We avoided lecturing you. We stopped threatening you with grounding or giving you more chores for breaking house rules.

We tried to remain nonjudgmental about your opinions and conclusions, and we learned to accept that there were no right answers. We were happy … as long as you stayed engaged in brief conversations about the purpose and meaning of school assignments. We dealt the same way with you about everyday behaviors, events, situations, observations, or conclusions you brought up.

We never asked you about your grades or progress in school, because we knew you could do well if you could think your way through assignments. We were excited that we had a way to communicate with you.

You began to do your homework with more interest, it seemed. You even told us how you challenged your teachers about the purpose of the assignments. When you got home from school, you shared snippets about your friends and your school day with us.

Phone calls from the principal and attendance office miraculously stopped.

At the end of the year, we were stunned to find out you had received As in all your subjects. You seemed excited to go on to college, and we were all momentarily overwhelmed when your teachers presented you with an extraordinary award at your graduation. You were named the "Come-Back Student of the Year."

Created especially for you or not, this award acknowledged a remarkable achievement.

When it's appropriate, I now tell this story to the parents I work with. I remind them that change is complex.

There are no simple answers to why you decided to change. Perhaps you were ready to change. Perhaps your maturing brain had developed a higher capacity to think, and you could better moderate your emotions. Indeed, I am certain that Mediated Learning helped. Maybe my study of Lao Tzu was also starting to work, at least on me.

The stars seemed to have aligned as we watched you learn how to learn.

We rejoiced that the method of Mediated Learning developed by the Israeli psychologist Reuven Feuerstein (1921–2014) worked. To paraphrase him, "If we could create experiences of mutual respect, curiosity, and delight at learning, all people could benefit."

A Letter to My Daughter

YOUR TURN TO REFLECT

How does your child learn best?

REFLECTION 16

KEEP THE LINES OF COMMUNICATION OPEN

I began thinking about the Eastern idea of "right action" to help prepare you for the world.

I constantly experimented, sought help from Eastern books, and went on spiritual retreats. The advice I had received from some Western books had worked when you children were young, but they needed adjustment, I thought, as you grew older. I could no longer give you choices between broccoli and brussels sprouts for dinner or give you time-outs when you broke a rule. I couldn't just give you more chores or withhold your privileges.

You had ideas of your own, and sometimes my feelings overrode my reasons. Sometimes all of our feelings did. We were a family and we had bonded with each other, whether we sometimes liked it or not. I once read that a family was like a rubber band expanding and contracting to accommodate its members. Ours certainly did.

When you and your brother were young, Dad and I had decided that if we only focused on communicating genuinely with you, our children, our whole family could be fine. We tried to do that ... but not always successfully. As you pushed against our rules, though, we began to try to incorporate your thoughts, ideas, and wishes. Through the experience of Mediated Learning and general negotiation, we often figured out how to come to a consensus without any of us walking away.

My family had a history of one person cutting off another family member when they disagreed. We had decided that this would not be an option for our own family, but I needed to develop a radar system to learn from you before you cut us off completely. I decided we should try some of the strategies from books I had already studied in my graduate counseling courses on parenting.

Dad and I decided when you were both quite young to adopt the "family council" concept into our family life. I learned from Rudolf Dreikurs, MD, in *Children: The Challenge* (1964) to turn individual situations into family problems that must be solved by the family together. All the members of the family needed to come to an agreement together. Parents could intervene, though, if or when the discussion becomes too heated or the emotions become too high.

Dad and I decided these discussions would be a way to develop trust and communication, and teach problem-solving within the family. We decided to implement family councils.

Your dad and I asked you two children to join us one night and, with all of us together, we began family council meetings to show you our commitment to communication. After that, we sat on the floor in a circle weekly to discuss any family concerns and how we could address them. We rotated the roles of discussion chair and recorder and made sure we recorded all decisions.

At several meetings when you were teens, you raised the subject of not wanting to do chores on the weekend. You said,

"We want more time with friends on the weekends. The chores take too much time!" You argued it was just our rule that on weekends we all did the laundry, vacuumed and dusted bedrooms and living rooms, and cleaned the bathroom, as well as did all the other chores involved in the upkeep of a home.

You didn't want to do chores that way anymore.

Dad and I acknowledged that you both had learned to keep a house clean—the only intent of these chores—so we had no reason to continue doing them ourselves, except perhaps to impress on you the discipline of keeping up a home and making you both feel part of a family. Finally, Dad and I suggested we hire a housekeeper, but we said you would both need to give up your allowances to do so. We couldn't afford the extra expense.

You readily agreed. The joy on your faces was priceless when we hired a housekeeper. You only had your personal laundry to do on the weekends, and you both found jobs for yourselves to replace your lost allowance.

I learned that making a mutual solution stopped any complaining. We had peace then in the family … well, at least about house cleaning.

Our family councils lasted until your brother graduated from high school and left for college, but now you both still ask for family council meetings when you want to raise a problem within the family.

Your continuing dedication to the family pleases your dad and me greatly. I am grateful that you trust us to know we are your family too.

Always with Much Love and Deep Aloha,
Mom

YOUR TURN TO REFLECT

What are some of the ways you have kept the lines of communication open with your children?

_____
_____
_____
_____
_____
_____
_____

Could you do more even with your adult children?

_____
_____
_____
_____
_____
_____
_____

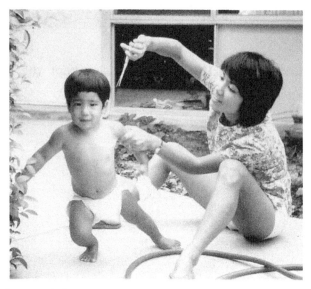

Sean aged about one: Tiger Mom trying to shape Sean's hair.

Sean about a year and a half, running to greet his dad when he returned from work.

Ann Yabusaki

Lee aged three and Sean aged six, forming a bond.

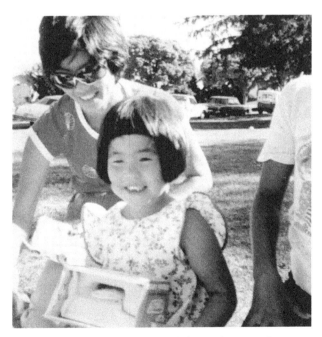

Lee aged three has her first birthday in the United States.

Lee aged four and Sean aged seven, goofing around on a family outing; both got car sick afterward.

Tiger Mom, Lee, and Sean, eating watermelon on the road.

Ann Yabusaki

Ann and Ken, Lee and Sean, taking a family photo at Christmas time.

A family Christmas photo when Lee was five and Sean was eight.

Sean and Lee are learning to get along.

Lee aged eight and Sean aged eleven, opening Christmas presents.

Ann Yabusaki

Picking Lee up from a horseback riding camp.

Sean and Lee are teenagers. They have been paying off their debt
—cleaning Mom and Dad's offices.

Ann Yabusaki

Lee is going to a dance aged thirteen; Sean's baseball game has finished.

Tiger Mom in 1987.

Happy Parents Ken and Ann at their fifty-third wedding anniversary.

Ann Yabusaki

From left to right, Lee, Ken, Tiger Mom, Sean,
and grandson Jacob in the back in 2022.

PART THREE

IT'S IMPOSSIBLE TO PROTECT MY CHILDREN FROM THE WORLD

> *Our lives begin to end the day we become silent about things that matter.*
>
> Martin Luther King, Jr.

Dearest Sean and Lee,

I wish we had spent more time talking about and explaining to you some of the challenges you both may have faced because of who you are and where you came from. We raised you in a world that was sometimes very hurtful because you were different than most people. You were Asian in a mostly white world.

Sean, I don't know why, but I think you, more than Lee, were targeted for your Asianness and differentness.

When at age eleven you had first wanted to earn money, we agreed to help you with a paper route. Early each morning before you went to school, Dad drove you on your paper route to deliver papers. One early dark morning, you saw a policeman crouching behind the fence on one of the main streets in town. You snuck up on him from behind.

"What are you doing?" you whispered to him.

The police officer, who was also your Little League Baseball coach jumped in surprise, but he recognized you and hugged you. He liked you and always told us you were one of his best players. You had no qualms either about talking with your high school baseball coach, who, like your Little League coach, happened to be Hispanic. Under them, you developed into an exceptional athlete and they admired your concentration and cooperation during practice and games.

You were an excellent athlete with good eye-hand coordination, and you had a love of physical sports. You swam competitively from the age of six through to eleven, and won many first and second places in freestyle and butterfly. When you played baseball for your high school the first year, you started in every game and could play several different positions. You even pitched a no-hitter.

Then, during your eleventh and twelfth grades, we noticed you rarely played baseball. We couldn't understand. Your Hispanic coach was no longer there. Dad would ask the new coaches why they weren't playing you, and later, he argued with them when the new coaches said that someone else was better and they just needed to win. One coach even claimed that you struck out too often, but Dad countered that only batting once in the last inning of a game was not a test of your abilities. You needed more playing time to improve.

I watched you cringe and look away whenever your dad argued with the coaches about letting you play more.

Then we began to notice the same pattern happening with the Black children. They were excellent athletes and had played often when the coach was Hispanic. They rarely played now with the new coach, who was white. Dad asked the fathers of the Black kids what was going on, because their kids, who were great players, were not playing.

The fathers laughed.

"It's the politics, man! It's the politics!" they responded bitterly.

Shocked, Dad whispered, "Do you mean racism?"

"Damn right!"

The African-American fathers shook their heads in mild despair when they saw Dad arguing with the coaches. They knew it would be of no use. No matter what Dad said, Sean, you would not get to play. The African-American fathers stayed behind the fence in the far outfield and watched their sons sitting on the bench with you.

Finally, one father confronted the white coach and threatened to sue the school due to racism. Then his son was allowed to play ball.

I felt the brunt of that implicit racism, as well. I felt the helplessness of not being able to protect you and your sister from it. After the Hispanic coach had left and you had white coaches, boys of color rarely played. You never talked to me about not playing, but I knew you overheard the coach tell your dad you weren't good enough.

Your dad and I felt helpless, watching you slump on the bench, head down, waiting patiently for your turn. We often talked to you and Lee about the situation to be sure that you both knew how wrong it was not to play you, Sean, explaining that you were an excellent player, and you were better than many of the others on the field. We wanted you to know that we believed in you, saw what was happening, and no longer denied the harsh reality of racism. I supported your dad as he continued to argue with the coaches even when you asked him not to. We tried our best to protect you.

YOUR TURN TO REFLECT

What are three values or beliefs you trying to pass on to your children?

What were some battles that you fought for your children?

REFLECTION 17

WHILE WE TRIED TO PROTECT YOU, OUR CHILDREN

In your twelfth grade, Sean, the principal called for a meeting with Dad and me. He claimed you and your friends were being racist on campus. As you explained to us, you had formed a group called WSU, the We Skate Union, and the group focused on skateboarding. The principal, though, interpreted the letters "WSU" as a disguise for the "white supremacist" students' union group taken from college campuses as the "White Student Union." The principal wanted it stopped immediately.

I was livid. Dad and I told the principal his accusation was wrong. I said I would take the matter to the superintendent if I had to.

I told him the school was racist. WSU did not stand for a white supremacist movement or a white student union.

I then repeated what Sean had said, "Many of the kids in the group are Asian, Hispanic, and Black, not White. How can they be part of a white supremacist movement?"

I pointed out that the school played minority students in sports infrequently. And these boys wanted their own nondiscriminatory sports group. I urged him to understand the politics of his school before accusing our son and his friends of racism.

Dad and I then made an appointment with the superintendent and presented our case to him.

The principal left the following year.

I felt compassion for him, for he was Hispanic and, I thought, was simply trying to run a politically "safe" school while being caught up in a white world.

Ironically, we had bought a home in this particular town because our realtor, who was Asian, had spoken so highly about the schools here. Many years later, our realtor told us that this town had once "redlined" Asians and Blacks so that realtors could not sell property in the city to minorities. Once redlining was made illegal in our town, our realtor and her husband were the first Asians to buy a home in the town. Like us, they wanted their children to have access to an excellent public education, but I'm sure their children suffered in school as you did.

You, first, and then, your sister, as well as the people of the town, showed me the devastating aggression of "isms" such as racism.

I wondered why it had taken me so long to understand all this. But until I dated your dad, I had only seen what it meant to be a person of privilege, not a minority. Because the majority of the people in Hawaii were of Asian descent, I was then seen as part of the "privileged people," the aggressors against the minority white people in Hawaii. Racism was subtle but insidious and so entrenched that I hadn't recognized myself as racist until I suffered what was, for me, the reverse discrimination of the mainland.

As parents, we were fighting for you and for ourselves.

YOUR TURN TO REFLECT

Were there times when you felt the need to protect your children?

_____
_____
_____
_____
_____
_____

What did you learn about yourself when trying to protect them?

_____
_____
_____
_____
_____
_____
_____

──── REFLECTION 18 ────

ABOUT THE PAST BEING THE PRESENT

In the middle of all your growing-up experiences, Dad and I learned more about "cultural barriers" when he had difficulty finding a job. After receiving his doctoral degree in biochemistry and finishing a post-doctoral position at a prestigious university in California, Dad wanted to teach. He sent applications to many colleges and universities throughout the US. Despite his stellar education, he was consistently rejected. We even initialized his Japanese first name and used his English middle name to help him appear "Western" so that he would "blend in."

When he still didn't get a job interview, he was so discouraged he thought of becoming a gardener as he had been in high school—the stereotypical Japanese-American profession. He even sold fish he caught to professors and staff at the university.

A few months later, Dad's former professor introduced him to another former student who knew a venture capitalist who was interested in starting a biotechnology research company. Dad presented his ideas of a new product and they expressed interest. He decided to partner with these men even though he didn't fully trust that they believed he could develop a research company. He often wondered whether people only considered him a good scientist because he fit the Asian stereotype of being the model minority and did not necessarily recognize his ideas and passion as being the reasons for his success.

Dad worked hard setting up the research laboratory—he found the space, scavenged and purchased used equipment from the university, installed the equipment, set up electrical outlets, and painted the laboratory while hiring and training technicians. Eventually, he had the laboratory running and the research was progressing smoothly. He arranged for a small company with an animal facility to make antibodies in rabbits for a medical test he was developing. Eventually, the test worked and the company patented the test.

Dad always had difficulty with the investors who wanted immediate results early on. They wanted to produce and market the test immediately, while Dad wanted to be sure it worked well before mass-producing and marketing it. Dad was angry and upset, and stressed for the next couple of years.

After over two years setting up Dad's company—while you, Sean, were in about fifth grade and Lee in second grade—the company fired Dad. He was hurt, angry, and resentful because the president hired another scientist to be Dad's boss without consulting Dad. Your dad was vice-president of research and an owner of the company, and he felt betrayed by the action. When Dad asked why they hired this other person, the president who had been financing the company said, "You're too quiet. You don't know how to speak like the guy we hired. He can make our investors smile in a minute!" He was implying that Dad wasn't "white or adept enough" at making investors feel comfortable.

The third partner said to Dad, "I never know what you're thinking."

"Why don't you ask me?" Dad asked sarcastically.

Dad's anger and resentment impacted us all. He filed for unemployment and had to prove that the firing was unfair. Your dad's scientific mind rose to the occasion, and he argued logically and successfully to the unemployment board that the firing was unjust. He became eligible for benefits. Dad was asked by other companies to consult on products, and the relationships always started out in a friendly and collaborative manner, but after a while he ended up arguing with all of the company presidents and left. And he again thought about becoming a gardener as he had been in high school. He completed a gardening project for a small business in our town.

Then he considered delivering pizzas. Both of you panicked at that idea and asked him not to deliver pizza because your friends' families would recognize him, and you didn't want them to know Dad couldn't find a "real" job.

By this time, Sean, you were getting into more trouble at school. The school almost daily called about you. And, Lee, you were smoking marijuana and cutting classes. I was clueless as to how to hold our family together.

Finally, when you were about eleven, Sean, you announced, "We need family therapy."

You wouldn't explain why, but I thought it was a great idea. Usually, children don't want therapy, so I was surprised yet again at your wisdom and willingness to speak up.

So we went.

Remember our first session?

We had to build a scene in a sandbox of what it was like to be in our family. We were supposed to represent our relationships

It's Impossible to Protect My Children from the World

with each other through miniature figures in a container the size of a kitty litter tray filled with sand.

Sean, you quickly took charge and Lee, eight years old, followed once she understood what she was supposed to do. There wasn't space for Dad and me to work next to you two, so we stood by and waited for our turn. I thought we'd also have a chance to put our figures into the tray, but there was no room for us in the tray after you two had finished.

You and your sister placed a miniature prince and princess in the middle of the tray, and then the two of you took all the miniature toy animals from the therapist's shelves and pointed their back ends toward the prince and princess standing in the middle.

Then you, Sean, roared with laughter and rolled on the floor, delighted with the scene, while your sister giggled, looking on. You gleefully pointed out to us what the figures were doing.

"In the center are the prince and princess," you said, "with the animals showing them their bare asses and making poo (passing gas) at them!"

We got the message.

We stopped family therapy, but Dad decided to talk to the therapist alone about all his falling-out with individuals in company relationships.

With the therapist's help, Dad realized that his family's internment camp experience, his parents' unwillingness to discuss it, and his early feelings for the government were all part of the hurt, betrayal, and anger he felt from being fired from his company. Racism was playing out in another painful form for him.

From this new insight, Dad fought the firing and the company compensated him handsomely. Dad kept his promise to always protect us.

YOUR TURN TO REFLECT

What would you tell your children about the past and future being in the present moment?

REFLECTION 19

DEVELOPING A PARENTAL VIEW IS CRITICAL

Your experience opened my eyes to the devastating impact of systemic racism and the accompanying politics of the town. From then on, I saw the school administration as targeting children of color, and I seethed with an anger I had never felt before. Your dad and I had always experienced racism, but when it happened to you and your sister, the "tiger mom" within me roared. I hadn't known it was there.

I vowed to speak for others if I could not get justice for you.

Dad and I joined and then became co-presidents of the local chapter of the Japanese American Citizens League, and for over twenty years participated fully in it. I later helped create a doctoral psychology program based on culture and the integration of diversity as a foundation for understanding the person. The students learned psychological theory, ethics, practice, and research, and they critiqued their learning from political, social, and cultural worldviews, as well as from their own personal points of view. Our family experience of the discrimination against you in high school fueled and shaped the rest of my life.

But, at the time, I felt there was little I could do immediately for you or your sister. As the high school years progressed and Dad and I experienced your anger, Sean, the wall of our denial fell about the ravages of racism on the human spirit, which we'd both seen. Try as we might, we couldn't stop it. All we could do was fight back in the best ways we knew at the time while we learned about the subtleties of racism and microaggression in our own neighborhood and their effects on the people in our community ... and particularly on the people closest to us, you and Lee.

Sean, because you and Lee were growing up as Asians in a white world—and I had not done that—I didn't realize how complex it would be for you and Lee to learn about your identity while living in a white culture from the start. I had at least grown up with my Asian ancestors and Asian mentors in Hawaii. I wish I had recognized earlier how you might have been feeling about who you were, and I had shared my own experiences with both of you so you wouldn't have felt so alone. Your stories reminded me of my own difficulties in accepting and integrating my cultural identity after moving to the mainland.

I now see I could have done far better to "accommodate" you, my own children. I can now see that there were at least two things I could have done that might have helped you and Lee through the racism you both experienced.

First, I should have told you both about Dad's and my own experiences growing up with racism, so that you'd see it was not about the two of you, in particular, being singled out as Asian youth. Racism has a longer history than that.

Second, I should have told you both far more of the story of your own Asian ancestors, so that you would have had a better idea of your cultural identity. If you had had a better understanding of the Asian traditions you had inherited—and could then have been proud to maintain—you might have had greater cultural self-confidence. Recognizing the strength of your Asian cultural identity might also have helped you better withstand the discrimination you ran up against during what was for each of you—as for any teenager—your difficult adolescent years when you were also trying to sort out your own individual identity.

Being racially different from those around you can cloud your whole life experience. It can give you your own identity, but it can also set you uncomfortably apart.

I have written a few stories in the next section of Dad's and my experiences, and experiences of your grandparents and great-grandparents so you'll know something about your past and the values with which you were raised. Take away whatever helps you to understand yourself and to always know you come from a line of resilient folks!

YOUR TURN TO REFLECT

Have you explained to your child, your children, the differences between themselves and others?

_____
_____
_____
_____
_____
_____

How did you or how do you decide if and when to explain that?

_____
_____
_____
_____
_____
_____
_____

―― REFLECTION 20 ――

MY LIFE OF EMBRACING A CULTURAL IDENTITY IS AS CHALLENGING AS A CATERPILLAR BECOMING A BUTTERFLY

Childhood Years

As you know, I was born and raised in Hawaii. You may not have known that approximately forty percent of the people in Hawaii at the time were Asian. Most of my teachers, bus drivers, counselors, and school administrators were Asian, Hawaiian, Portuguese, Filipino, and mixtures of many more ethnic cultures. There may have been more, but I remember only two white and one Black student in my high school of three thousand students.

Because I grew up as part of the "majority," I didn't think of myself as Asian, nor did I feel I was racist. I now see that I was part of the privileged majority.

Then, in fifth grade, I learned Hawaiian history and its history of colonialism. Although I was of Asian descent, I felt a deep connection to this land, Hawaii, and embraced its history as my own. The story of Hawaii left me with a wave of anger that still influences me today. The United States invaded our islands, imprisoned our queen, and annexed Hawaii—our land—as a territory of the United States. Queen Liliuokalani was my first symbol of a conscientious objector who fought for freedom. Missionaries and business people colonized Hawaii, became the *lunas* (the bosses of the plantations, ranches, and businesses) and forbade the practices of Hawaiian culture, language, and customs.

I wondered, as a high school student, why Hawaii appeared to be governed by white men when Hawaii was predominantly inhabited by Asian, Hawaiian, Portuguese, and other people of color. How was this possible?

College Years

I decided to attend a small private college in the Midwest—where I would be one of very few Asians—so I could learn about the white culture's values, language, and thoughts, and experience how they lived and what was important to them. I wanted to understand the cultures of the mainland to better understand how to be in and relate to the majority culture.

When I received a modest work-study scholarship from this college, my father reluctantly allowed me to go. He wanted me to remain in Hawaii, attend the local university and become a teacher. I, however, wanted to become a psychologist and study people.

I had never before flown on an airplane and I had never been to the mainland. When I arrived, I was awestruck by the beautiful campus with its red brick buildings and stone chapel, sitting at the top of a hill. In Hawaii, I had never seen red-brick buildings. The buildings surrounded a beautiful grassy "Quad," a field the size of a football field, which sloped gently from the top of the hill to the bottom, where the boys' dormitories were located. It was a stunning campus—covered with green grass in the warm months and with ice and snow during the winter. I had never seen snow and was mesmerized by it. I slipped and fell on the ice until I learned about boots and walking on cleared sidewalks.

I learned on arrival that I would be one of only two or three Asian students on campus.

I quietly entered the white world. I gave up rice for potatoes, ate with a fork instead of chopsticks, and learned to set the table with forks, knives, and spoons instead of chopsticks, rice bowls, and small dishes for the food placed family style in the center of the table. I learned to participate in "small talk," a way of speaking about nothing on my mind, as a way of socializing. I trained myself to focus my gaze on people's eyes as I spoke. A friend told me that shifting my gaze away from the face of a person I was speaking with seemed as if I was hiding something, even though it traditionally means deference and respect in Asian culture. I forced myself to share opinions and question my professors in class, breaking the "rule" of children learning by observation and imitation. I had to speak directly to feel understood and I used few if no metaphors or stories. The indirectness of my Asian roots had little place on the mainland.

Everyone seemed so confident and sure of themselves that I wondered if they ever doubted what they said. I rarely spoke up in class because I couldn't think or enter into the pauses as quickly as the white students did. Everything was too fast.

Once, when I was brave enough to jump in, one of my professors told me, "I appreciate your finally speaking up!"

My roommate showed me how to dress, lent me her clothes so I could blend in, and showed me how to apply makeup. She taught me what to talk about and how a girl behaved when on a date with a boy. The girls in the dormitory always talked about dating and boys in general, so I learned quickly. I had no dating experience.

My books became my dates and companions, and I was determined not to fail. When I arrived, I was self-conscious about speaking pidgin English, and deliberately and conscientiously practiced speaking standard English.

Those college years challenged my beliefs and values, and forced me to re-define who I was. Most adolescents struggle with identity in high school. I struggled with it in college. *If I don't think, behave, speak, or believe like my classmates, then who am I?* I tried to "adapt" to the environment by imitating others, but I knew something was wrong and often wondered if there was something wrong with me. I had never felt so isolated and lonely before and I believed something was wrong with me.

These years were the most depressing years of my life.

In my first year, I befriended a custodian in the college cafeteria, a grandfatherly man from Latvia, who tried to help me with my transition. I cleared dishes and cleaned tables, and he showed me around the cafeteria, explaining how things worked. He probably knew I was lost, and he tried to be kind. He invited me to his home, and his wife made a special Latvian cake for tea. They shared stories with me about their homeland, coming to America, and their experiences adjusting to the United States.

I wish I had made more effort to be as friendly with them as they were with me, but I was overwhelmed with the environment, traumatized by the differences I felt with others, and depressed because nothing was familiar. I didn't feel as though I had an identity.

My Junior Year Abroad

As part of my college's curriculum, I could choose where to study abroad during my junior year. I decided to spend my foreign study year in Japan, hoping to learn more about my own roots. I studied Japan's language and culture during my freshman and sophomore years. I also studied the German language, in case I wasn't admitted into the program in Japan. I had never been to Japan and, when I was accepted, I was excited to be immersed in "my" culture and to learn "who I am." As part of the experience, I lived on a farm during the summer with a Japanese-speaking family, learning to care for cows, plant rice in the fields, and work with the goats. After the summer, I lived in a suburb of Tokyo with a young Japanese couple who had three lovely children aged two, three, and four. No one spoke English, so I had to practice and learn Japanese. I took a train to a university in Tokyo to attend classes for international studies. During my holidays, I explored Japan and was thrilled to visit places I had only read about in books and brochures.

The first time I entered a Japanese train station, I descended the stairs to the boarding platforms and became confused because all the signs were in Japanese. I couldn't read as well as I could speak, so I wasn't sure which platform I needed to be on for my train.

When I asked the station master if I was correct, he answered, "What's the matter? Can't you read?" and walked away.

"I am an American!" I yelled, to explain my ignorance, but he shook his head and walked away without looking back.

When I wore a kimono given to me by my Japanese family, people on the street sometimes commented, "You're not Japanese!" as if to scold me for pretending to be Japanese.

If I wasn't a Japanese in Japan and wasn't an American in America, then who was I?

I felt different, no matter where I went. I did not "fit in." Angry, I began saying, "I am from Hawaii, not America." Somehow, saying that, I felt more welcomed by the people in Japan and at my college.

One of my best friends in college was Joe, a boy from an Italian family living in Chicago. We both took our study-abroad year in Japan. I asked Joe if I could travel through Japan with him during our school breaks because I wanted to see the country, and I knew I would have a better time if I traveled with a handsome *gaijin* (Japanese for pale-eyed foreigner).

He agreed and it was true: I was treated well when I traveled with Joe. I saw the country and appreciated his protection throughout our journey.

At the end of four years of college, I was tired of trying on all these new ways, and I longed to be among people who were more like me. I wanted to rest and I wondered why people from other cultures did not try to accommodate me.

When it was time for me to graduate from college, seniors were required to take the Graduate Record Examination and pass with a particular score in their major. I took the exam, scored below the passing cutoff, and worried I wouldn't graduate.

It's Impossible to Protect My Children from the World

A few days later, my professor asked me to meet her in her office to discuss my performance. I was frightened, but she reassured me that I would graduate.

"I understand you're from Hawaii," she said, "and that makes a difference."

She was from Canada and confided that she also had difficulty understanding American culture. I remember her saying, "The standardized tests are biased against people from different cultures or from rural areas, because underlying the tests are cultural assumptions that others may not share. Hence, you are disadvantaged when taking these national tests."

For the first time, I felt seen.

I hadn't realized until then that I had felt I was invisible. My professor's explanation helped clarify my experience of being immersed as Asian in a white culture that was American. I had unsuccessfully tried to imitate the other students and had secretly wondered what was wrong with me, but no one had ever told me I was different. Everyone treated me as if I were the same as them, yet I knew I was not.

That "gift" from my professor put four years of confusion into perspective. I could open my eyes to the damaging process of racism—to "isms" in general—to invisibility and to the myth that "we are all alike."

I saw for the first time that I had my own identity.

I immediately applied for graduate school to study cultural anthropology and the psyche, and to familiarize myself with a new understanding of psychology. I also wanted to explore the Japanese-American experience in mainland US and learn how they handled racism so I could address it in my life better. I wanted mentors.

Graduate School

I was accepted at a university in Seattle, Washington, and immersed myself in the study of cultures and the Japanese-American experience. I met many people from the Japanese-American community, including your dad, and I learned about Japanese-Americans' internment experiences during World War II.

Forty years after the closure of those camps, I could not find any adults willing to talk about their experiences there. Like many other Japanese-Americans, my mother-in-law just dismissed it with *shikata ga nai* (Japanese for "it can't be helped;" "let go;" "accept what you cannot change") and *gaman* (Japanese for "endure with patience and dignity"). To me, her dismissals of my outrage at the incarceration meant "don't complain."

Nothing Prepared Me for Parenting in a Different Culture

Living on the mainland, I protected myself against everyday racist aggression by denying and deflecting it, imitating my classmates and mainland ways to blend in—like speaking directly and concisely and shortening the pause between people in conversations, making firm eye contact when speaking, and dressing, walking and sitting like a Westerner. I learned to work with and around diverse worldviews strategically.

When I became a parent, though, I was unprepared to protect you both. Nothing had alerted me or prepared me for the difficulties of parenting in a racist system. If I had been honest with myself when I had to deal with the discrimination you two faced, I would have realized that sometimes my motives were still more about trying to "look good" as a parent or a person, and less about your personal circumstances.

It has hurt me deeply to see how my inadequacy might then have hurt you. Throughout your childhoods, Dad and I often discussed *What can we do to protect you? How can we help you grow up to love yourselves?*

I remember how we wanted you both to have a close relationship with your grandparents. We wanted you to know where you came from, their history, struggles, and stories. We forgot to tell you that their values were passed down to you and that you would have to find some way to blend the culture that you faced every day in the neighborhood with the culture of your ancestors.

YOUR TURN TO REFLECT

How did your past prepare you for parenting?

REFLECTION 21

MY GRANDPARENTS AND PARENTS

Your Hawaii Great-Grandparents

My grandparents, your maternal great-grandparents, came to Hawaii from Okinawa, the southernmost island of Japan. Your dad's father, your paternal grandfather, emigrated to Seattle from Hiroshima, Japan, when he was eighteen. He later met and married your grandmother. Your grandmother's parents, too, had emigrated to Seattle from Hiroshima, Japan. So, a heavy influence of traditional Japanese values, beliefs, customs, and worldviews came down through our families to you.

I realize now that you both showed us these values throughout your lives, but I failed earlier to see that.

Your great-grandparents in Hawaii, *Baba* (Japanese for "grandmother") and *Jiji* (Japanese for "grandfather") emigrated from Okinawa in the late 1800s to work in Hawaii's sugarcane and pineapple fields. They initially lived on sugarcane plantations in Ewa, on Oahu's leeward side, and later moved to the Kalihi district of Honolulu. They somehow purchased several plantation-style homes on a large property where my aunties and uncles lived with their families.

Eventually, some of my uncles and aunts moved out, and Jiji rented out three homes. He and Baba lived upstairs in a two-story, three-bedroom house on the property and rented the downstairs to my *calabash* auntie (Hawaiian for a person who is close but not biologically related).

I was a little girl when I visited Baba and Jiji's home. I remember Baba's tiny bedroom off the kitchen, where she cooked for the family; I remember she cooked all kinds of dishes for her lunch wagon business. Jiji slept in a room off the dining room where they stored Baba's supplies for her business. They ate on a small picnic table in the kitchen. An old washer and hand-wringer dryer were outside under the house's eaves, and clotheslines hung between two T-posts in the backyard. A picture of Buddha hung in the living room, and a picture of Jesus Christ hung in a third bedroom off the living room.

Baba and Jiji made *sake* (a Japanese wine) under their house during the prohibition years and gave some to friends. They were determined to live life "their" way. During World War II, the FBI visited their family often because the Japanese were considered spies. When Grandpa saw them coming, he hid the picture of Buddha in the living room and put up the one of Christ.

The back of the house rested on stilts because the backyard gently sloped toward a mountain stream. Jiji was a carpenter and he stored his tools and work projects under that part of the house. Stone walls lined each side of a stream so that there was safety for everyone when it rained and the stream swelled into a rapidly flowing river.

Baba raised chickens, and grew green onions and other vegetables in the backyard on the slope. One day my mother brought me for a visit to Baba. She was in the backyard, and

It's Impossible to Protect My Children from the World

I raced downstairs but stopped abruptly. Baba held the head of a squirming chicken with one hand and a huge knife in the other; she was poised to cut off its head. She did so and let the bird go. It ran in circles, spurting blood everywhere. She then grabbed it again, threw it into a large galvanized garbage can, covered it, and listened for the bird to stop banging against the can's walls. Once it was quiet, she pulled the chicken out, grabbed it by the neck, and, holding it away from her, began to pluck off its feathers.

I watched, horrified.

She must have done this many times because she laughed at me for gagging throughout the ordeal while she removed the feathers and gutted and cleaned the chicken. Afterward, she brought it upstairs into the kitchen, cut it into pieces, and fried it for supper in a wok.

I ate some of it, and it was delicious.

However, the death of that chicken was embedded in my memory forever. That day, Baba had taught me—whether she knew it or not—that you do what you must do to survive.

Baba created one of the first lunch wagons in Hawaii. She drove out to the pineapple and sugarcane fields in Ewa and sold hot *bento* (Japanese box lunches) to the workers. Baba's truck was much like an old UPS truck, except it was white and it opened up on the side with a window from where she sold her food. She sold *tempura* (batter-fried vegetables and shrimp served with sauce), fried chicken, *nishime* (a Japanese stew over white rice), macaroni salad, and *andagi* (Okinawan doughnuts).

I loved her cooking and often ate some of it at her kitchen table while watching her cook. She laughingly scolded me for eating her profits, but she always had a warm smile for everyone.

I have no idea how she got her driver's license without knowing English well, but she acquired the truck and a business license to start her business. She stood up while driving because she couldn't reach the pedals when sitting. Her determination, always with a smile, taught me that life doesn't have to be a burden.

I've seen that determination in both of you, too, my children.

Your Hawaii Grandma's Story

My mother, your grandmother, was born in Oʻokala, a rural community on the Big Island of Hawaii, where schooling ended in the tenth grade. She enjoyed learning and was disappointed that she would have to go to Honolulu on the island of Oahu to complete her high school diploma. As a young adult, she went to live with her older brother in Honolulu to work. She later met and married my father, your grandfather, and they had three children together—your two uncles and me. While working full-time and raising three young children, she attended adult night school for her General Education Diploma (GED), which is equivalent to a high school diploma. About ten years after leaving Oʻokala, she graduated as the class valedictorian and gave an inspirational speech that she saved for us to read. I kept it for you.

She then went on to technical school to receive her certification as an X-ray technician. Despite achieving her certification and becoming chief of the X-ray department at one of Hawaii's major hospitals, your grandmother felt inferior because she only had a GED, despite the fact that it was equivalent to a high school diploma. Still, throughout her career, she would argue with the white physicians about their demeaning and demanding attitude toward the non-white support staff most of whom had high school diplomas, good educations at the time.

Your grandmother complained when the white doctors brought only a small bowl or plate of food to share at the department's potluck luncheons while eating the most and then leaving. She could not make them understand that the Polynesian-Asian custom of bringing generous portions of food so people could take leftovers home to share with their families was as important as the food itself. The tradition of feeding each other is part of *Aloha*.

Your grandmother's frustration and resentment became a part of me as I learned to judge other people with her values. It wasn't much later that I wondered why some people felt the right to infringe on others' values at all.

Despite her frustration with cultural differences, your grandmother attended a Christian church. I attended it with her throughout my school years, and I enjoyed the sermons, hymns, and people there. I was comfortable knowing there is a God. I also felt drawn to my grandparents' philosophy of the Buddha, Tao, and Confucian philosophies and I never thought they conflicted with my Christian upbringing. I was familiar with these philosophies because your grandparents, great-grandparents, and ancestors all came from Okinawa. They showed me a way of thinking and living that was different from the American perspective I would later learn.

So, although I went to a Christian church in my own youth, I've often thought about my father's and his parents' Buddhist beliefs in the Spirit as I pursued my own Eastern spiritual studies during these last years. I'm sure Dad and I passed on an integrated philosophy to you.

Your Hawaii Grandpa's Story

Grandpa was born in the sugarcane fields of Ewa, Hawaii. He was educated in Okinawa, Japan, from age five through seventeen because it was the custom for children to be educated in their home country. At the same time, they cared for their family members who had remained in Okinawa. His first language was Japanese, so I had to learn his way of communicating. He was more Okinawan at heart than American and I now realize the stories he told me were to teach me about life, family, and parenting.

Children born in Hawaii, raised in Okinawa, and later returned to Hawaii as adults were known as *kibbei*. The *kibbei* formed Okinawan clubs and entertainment groups in Hawaii, and they supported each other in their Okinawan identity as they integrated into an American-Hawaiian society. They became Japanese language teachers, priests, businessmen, and shop owners; they opened authentic Japanese restaurants for the community; and they formed clubs for cultural support.

During World War II, they became decoders and interpreters for the American army. They formed the Okinawan Society and helped to build the Hawaii Okinawa Center that opened in 1990. After the war, the *kibbei* organized shipments of clothing, pigs, food, and other necessities to send to Okinawa to help rebuild the communities from which they came.

Your grandfather was one of the first presidents of the United Okinawa Association of Hawaii and he helped to build the Hawaii Okinawa community center. He was an intelligent and gentle man, and many of his friends and acquaintances would ask him to write letters to their families to introduce them to women in Okinawa. They wanted picture brides to begin families, and they felt Grandpa was a poet who could convince families with daughters to arrange marriages for them. The Okinawan community helped each other like that. Grandpa also brought electricity to his village in Okinawa after the war, because of his relationship with the US Army.

Your grandpa and grandma later moved in with his parents, Baba and Jiji, to care for them until their deaths.

Dad and I were staying with Grandma and Grandpa when we attended Jiji's funeral. A couple of nights after Jiji died, Grandpa told me he woke up with a start.

"I saw Jiji at the foot of my bed, smiling at me," he told us the following day. "I think he was telling me everything was okay. When I went to the kitchen to make coffee, the back door was open. I checked with Mom, but she said she didn't leave it open! Did you?"

We were preparing breakfast and were startled by his story. "No," we said, and we too wondered why the door was open.

We never spoke about spirits or the afterlife or even this incident again. I think Jiji showed up to tell Grandpa that he was pleased and that he had forgiven him for returning to Hawaii before the war. I think Jiji knew that the family in Okinawa had sent Grandpa home before the war because he would have been conscripted into the Japanese military if he had stayed. Forgiveness was such a strong part of our culture that someone would even return from the dead to make sure another knew they had been forgiven.

YOUR TURN TO REFLECT

What are some reasons to tell or not tell your children about their past?

_____

_____

_____

_____

_____

_____

What do your answers tell you about your values?

_____

_____

_____

_____

_____

_____

_____

_____

_____

REFLECTION 22

YOUR GRANDPA IN HAWAII

Fierce Independence Is Necessary for Living a Successful Life

A few years after we moved in with your grandfather to care for him, your dad and I asked him not to drive anymore. He was eighty-eight years old, and we worried about his driving ability.

One afternoon, we left on an errand. When we returned, Grandpa greeted us at the door with a big grin.

"I went driving to the market!" he told us.

"What!"

I could feel my blood pressure rise with anger.

"Don't be mad. Don't be mad. Don't be mad!" Grandpa teasingly sing-songed to me as he followed me into the kitchen.

I smiled and knew he had me. How could I remain angry when all he wanted was his freedom? Still, I worried.

I finally understood the importance of freedom and felt guilty for and conflicted between keeping him and others safe on the road while still giving him a sense of autonomy. That sounds like some of my conflict trying to be a disciplined but permissive parent to you, doesn't it?

Children Are Gold

After I had gone to college on the mainland, on a rare visit with your grandpa, he and I sat in the living room talking about what I was doing at graduate school.

Suddenly, peering at me over his glasses, he said, "My friend told me I was a rich man!"

"What did he mean?" I asked, confused.

"Children doing well is gold to a parent! So, he said I am a rich man!"

I looked at him, wondering whether he thought that was true. From the outside, we might look like a "good" family—whatever that meant—but inside, I was still struggling to understand the people and culture on the mainland. As for being a rich family ... we were always poor financially.

It wasn't easy for me then to understand a parent's perspective, but I now understand what my father's friend meant. What matters in life to a parent is that their children are safe and doing well. I knew that your grandpa was proud of his children and loved us deeply. We were all gold to him.

I hope you realize, Sean and Lee, that you are gold to Dad and me.

When I returned home after graduate school, Grandpa and I sat in the living room again.

"Did I ever tell you what happened when my friend visited while you were in college?" he asked.

"No," I said.

"My friend stopped by with a bag of oranges. He wanted to talk about you and to know if you had a boyfriend. He asked if I would consider his son for you."

"What!" I was shocked. I thought the Japanese tradition of a *baishakunin* (Japanese for a "go-between" or a "matchmaker") no longer existed.

"I felt insulted," your grandpa said to me.

Then he burst out laughing.

"I told him, no! You're worth more than a bag of oranges!"

Parents from an Asian culture never tell their children they love or are proud of them. They never celebrate good grades and achievements because they raise their children to be humble. Their language is contextual and indirect, so it's sometimes hard to know what people mean. Grandpa had told me how proud of me he was by telling me these stories.

So, when I did not comment on your doing well, it did not mean I was not proud of you. I was. I was just following the Japanese values from my own upbringing.

Cultural Protocols Are Important

When Dad and I returned to Hawaii to live with and care for your grandpa, we cooked, cleaned, shopped, and took him to medical appointments and occasionally out to eat. At home one day, I decided to take a short break from all these activities, and I asked Grandpa if he wanted to eat the last ice cream bar in the freezer.

He was sitting in his usual chair in the TV room, watching the news from Japan, and he looked up at me and said, "No."

"Okay," I said.

I grabbed the bar from the freezer and sat at the bottom of the stairwell, facing him, intending to keep him company.

As I unwrapped the ice cream, he yelled, "Stop! What are you doing?"

"Huh? I'm eating the ice cream."

"Whassa matta you! You're supposed to ask me three times before you eat the ice cream! What kinda Japanese, you?"

"Oh," I replied meekly. Now I understood why he was so upset.

"Okay," I smiled, recognizing the protocol. "Would you like the ice cream bar?"

"No, thank you!" he responded and peered at me over his glasses.

"Would you like to eat the last ice cream bar?" I asked him again.

"Yes. Thank you!" he said, grinning like the Cheshire cat and motioning me to give it to him. I handed it over reluctantly.

We create relationships only through the practice of cultural protocol, no matter what our culture is. Sometimes those protocols conflict with each other.

I learned about another protocol at your wedding, Lee. Your grandpa felt *haji* (Japanese for "shame") because your first son was born out of wedlock. I don't know if you, your fiance, or Sean understood Grandpa's feelings about children and marriage. When he learned that your son, his five-year-old great-grandson, would be at the wedding, he panicked about how to introduce the boy ... when you were not yet married.

He was so distressed that Grandpa took your dad and me aside privately.

"Can't we hide him?" he asked.

Hide him at the wedding!

I thought Grandpa was joking.

He was serious. I stammered and panicked and did not know what to say.

"No, we can't!" I finally blurted out. "He's the ring bearer!"

There were far too many conflicts of cultural protocol and wedding etiquette in that one little moment with your grandpa for me to handle. I had blown up at him.

If I'd remembered that incident when the two of you and I were later having some of our "cultural protocol" conflicts, I might not have flown so far off the handle at times, especially since you were already adults.

YOUR TURN TO REFLECT

Identify three cultural protocols in which you were raised.

_____
_____
_____
_____
_____
_____
_____

If you wanted to, which of those cultural protocols would you tell your children about?

_____
_____
_____
_____
_____
_____
_____

PARENTING IS CHALLENGING IN ANY LANGUAGE

Grandpa rarely scolded us as children, but he seemed to lose his English when he did. One day, when I was a young girl, I refused to mop the floors when he asked me to because I wanted to finish reading a book. He began chasing me around the house and finally stopped in the living room, fuming and red-faced.

"Ugly girl!" he yelled at me.

I laughed at him. He stormed out the front door and wouldn't talk to me for the rest of the day. That was the only time I remember him scolding me, but now I'm ashamed that I secretly laughed at his English because all he knew to say was, "Ugly girl!"

YOUR TURN TO REFLECT

Were there moments in your parenting (or your parents' parenting of you) that left you or them speechless?

_____

_____

_____

_____

_____

_____

_____

How do you feel, recalling those moments?

_____

_____

_____

_____

_____

_____

_____

REFLECTION 23

YOUR DAD'S EXPERIENCE OF HAWAII

Your dad was born in Minidoka, Idaho, in the Japanese American internment camp at the end of World War II and raised in Seattle. He and I met in Seattle when I was a graduate student at the university, three weeks before he left to serve in the army. He had never visited Hawaii and arrived there a few days before our wedding.

I didn't realize how different it was for him until he started telling me what he noticed.

The bathroom floor of our house in Hawaii sagged from termite damage, and Dad noticed that Grandpa had installed braces under the toilet to keep it from falling through the floor.

"I never before saw the dirt under a house while taking a piss!" Dad commented after first entering our home. He was actually impressed with the jacks that Grandpa used to reinforce the flooring of the toilet and bathtub.

Dad was also startled to find only a single light bulb hanging from the ceiling to light up the kitchen; he was fascinated, while washing the dirty dishes in the kitchen, to watch the neighbors across the street through the kitchen window. They were smoking marijuana and sniffing glue in their open garage.

Even if the walls were thin, the wood termite-eaten, and the rooms small and cluttered, it was our home, and my family and I had never thought about living differently. That was before I had begun fully integrating myself—or trying to—into American culture.

Dad noticed that although he was Japanese-American, the experience in Hawaii was far different from what he had expected. He asked me to interpret when he couldn't understand the thick pidgin English of the gas station attendants ("You no change the oil, you gotta cho-way your engine!"); they laughed at his lack of understanding. He thought it was a clever way of communicating and imitated speaking in pidgin to learn the language. He loved being treated with respect wherever he went and noticed how he didn't have to spell or repeat his name because there were so many Asians in Hawaii. He looked like everyone else and "fitted in." He said, "People are really nice!"

YOUR TURN TO REFLECT

Recall a time when you felt very different from others. What did you notice about yourself?

How might this experience of being different influence your parenting?

——— REFLECTION 24 ———

YOUR SEATTLE GRANDPARENTS' STORY

After I met your dad, I learned more about his family. I want to share a little about his family here to help you understand that their experience is also part of you.

Part of the experience of racism experienced by your dad's family (parents, maternal grandparents, and your dad's older sister) started when they lost their home because of the forced relocation to the concentration camp in Minidoka, Idaho, during World War II. They were initially taken by bus from Seattle to Puyallup, Washington, where they lived at a fairground in empty horse stables that reeked of horse urine and manure. There they waited for several months before boarding trains to Minidoka. They were incarcerated for three years as "enemy aliens" in this country. Your dad was born there. He and his family, Japanese-American prisoners of war, were released nine months later.

However, in the forty years I've known them, no one on your dad's side of the family ever spoke about their internment experiences. Like many other Japanese-Americans, your grandparents dismissed it with *shikata ga nai* (it can't be helped; let go; accept what you cannot change) and *gaman* (endure with patience and dignity), as I said, meaning "Why talk about it?" They seemed to say, "Let's move on." Dad and I, like many of the younger generation who were not interned or were interned at a very young age, could only imagine what it must have been like to be uprooted, treated as enemies in your own country, and then released to build a new life where people continued to treat you as the enemy.

That was their cultural protocol for handling a "difficulty" in life. I know you've also seen me use those cultural values after upsets with you, and—no matter how you ended up inheriting it—you've used the same *shikata ga nai* (it can't be helped; let go; accept what you cannot change) with me after some of our blowups.

I have displayed and therefore passed on other values from our Japanese ancestry to you. I have shown you and thus taught you, even if subconsciously, *gaman* (endure with patience and dignity) and *enryo* (Japanese for being restrained, humble, modest). To me these cultural terms mean "to blend into the environment." In an American culture, such as the one you grew up in, these Japanese values take on both a positive and a negative aspect. *Gaman* may mean being culturally polite, but it also promotes holding oneself back from speaking when it's actually important to let another know what you're feeling. Likewise, it is fine to practice *enryo*, but not when being so humble makes you invisible and suppresses your ability to be satisfied with your accomplishments.

I did try to teach you *oyakoko* (Japanese for "respect for parents") as I tried to respect your spirit. I knew that my family was always my priority and that my *on* (Japanese for "kindness"; to me it meant "obligation") was to you. I may not have been perfect at balancing work and family life, but I was always aware that our family—every generation of it, from my grandparents to my children—was part of my identity. I want *Okage sama de* (Japanese for "because of you, I am") to be part of your identity too, because it will stabilize you in a world now unsteady in its cultural certainties.

I just wish I had done more of this earlier.

I believe, too, that while our Japanese ancestry may have been unfairly put into the spotlight as discrimination, even as racism, any parent will find that the "cultural" protocols and values they have subconsciously learned from their ancestors will give their children a meaningful identity. It will also set them up to be seen as "different." Unfortunately, that difference can be tipped over into discrimination, regardless of one's ethnic background.

I have found in my counseling practice that every parent can benefit from being made aware of both the positive and negative values of making their own family identity known to their children.

Finally, my children, know that both of you possess the traits of courage and of compassion, just like your grandparents and great-grandparents and Dad. I can see that these traits are transmitted through the generations, and I'm grateful that you're both like the family in which you were raised. I wish I had pointed that out to you more as you were growing up, but I didn't know it was so important then.

I now know that parents cannot protect their children against racism and the complexities of developing an identity … including a cultural identity. The best we can do is enroll our children in more equitable schools, redirect and support their energies into proactive activities, help them embrace and appreciate their ancestors and who they are, reflect on what they do well, discuss the complex issues of differences and discrimination honestly and openly, and let them know they are gold!

And that's what we tried to do … but we could have done more, done it earlier, and maybe, done it better.

Always with Much Love and Aloha,
Mom

YOUR TURN TO REFLECT

What, if any, history about your family would you convey to your children?

_____
_____
_____
_____
_____
_____

Do you sometimes feel as though your family's history is repeating itself in your or your children's lives?

_____
_____
_____
_____
_____
_____

PART FOUR

LETTING YOU GO REQUIRES COURAGE

To hold, you must first open your hand. Let go.

Lao Tzu

My Dearest Sean and Lee,

When you became adults and moved out of the home and into making your own lives, Dad and I realized that we had to change our parenting style. It was confusing for us because we asked, "How do we parent children who no longer live with us making their own decisions without our input!?" We had to accept that we would learn about your lives by what you decided to tell us. We worried in silence and for me, prayer became a large part of parenting!

---------- REFLECTION 25 ----------

THE FINAL EXAM OF PARENTING

What I was not prepared for was your venturing into drugs and alcohol at college, Sean, and being arrested and jailed for a week. Fortuitously, Dad headed a company near your college at that time. He rented an apartment nearby so he could visit you often, and only came home on weekends.

Dad told me that on one occasion when he visited you, he was so angry and disappointed that he asked you, "What did I do wrong for you to do what you're doing?"

"You're just being a dad, Dad," you sighed and then gave Dad a high-five—a loving open hand hug—against the glass window that separated the two of you at the jail. Dad returned his hand while holding back his tears.

Despite your circumstances, you had drawn a cartoon of a young man holding a picket sign saying, "Let Sean Out!" Dad shared the drawing with me when he got home and told me you were giving your desserts to the "alpha inmate" to buy protection. You told Dad that you stayed quiet in your cell, tried not to make eye contact with others, and read books as you waited to get out of jail.

My anger and disappointment about your selling drugs slowly faded as I watched you take responsibility for your behavior. Dad, being nearer you while renting the apartment, discreetly kept an eye on you, but his precaution proved unnecessary. Drugs were out of the picture for you, though you continued to drink alcohol with your friends.

After a panicked trip to the emergency room and a week in the hospital for an inflamed pancreas, you finally stopped drinking altogether.

During those years, we never left you … even as you had drifted into the Dark Night of the Soul. I always prayed to ask the angels to watch over you; I prayed for miracles as you tried to find your way.

Then you left that lifestyle altogether. Your dad and I had trusted you to figure all that out for yourself, even though he and I were often nervous wrecks while we waited for you to do so.

YOUR TURN TO REFLECT

What parallels are there between your growing up and your children's?

_____
_____
_____
_____
_____
_____
_____

What do you think you taught them?

_____
_____
_____
_____
_____
_____
_____

REFLECTION 26

CHILDREN FIND THEIR PATH IN THEIR OWN WAYS

After that, Sean, you worked selling magazines and at a photocopying shop, you lost your girlfriend, and then you finally dropped out of college. You ventured into the business of providing audiovisual and technical support at conferences, and you made many good and loyal friends. I still remember how you set up three conferences I was in charge of and worked on two of them by yourself. Even today, your willingness to volunteer at the conferences I do impresses me.

You now watch your health, you have taught yourself to work on computers, you continue to freelance at conferences, you've cultivated wonderfully loyal friends, and you've built a loving community for yourself among them. You have taken responsibility for your life.

All of that brings great comfort to us.

YOUR TURN TO REFLECT

If your dreams for your children were different from their dreams for themselves, how did you reconcile that difference?

― REFLECTION 27 ―

GROWING MY SELF

As I said earlier, I turned to books on meditation, spiritual healing, prayer, miracles, and Buddhism throughout all this time. For over forty years, I have searched for spiritual answers because I knew all my education about the mind was not enough, but I didn't know how to access those higher realms. Being a caring parent forced me to seek answers both within and beyond reason.

The lesson of letting go means not only letting go of you and your sister, but also letting go of my beliefs, my assumptions, my presumptions, and my academic learning. As a parent, I had to let go of being ashamed, embarrassed, and self-critical. As a perfectionist, I had to let go of trying to be "perfect."

Through parenting and participating fully in our family, I have learned to let go of predictability and of forceful attempts to control you or your sister. I have let go of my fear and worry about the worst possible outcome, and I have learned to ask the heavenly helpers to help you, to send love, and to begin to trust my heart and my intuition. Most of all, I have learned to forgive myself for being such a "controlling Tiger Mom."

And I am still learning self-compassion. Thank you, Sean, for the gift you are.

YOUR TURN TO REFLECT

Reflecting back over the years, what did your children show you about yourself?

REFLECTION 28

DESPITE OUR WISHES, WE NEED TO LET GO

Lee, once we settled you into your dormitory near the campus, we never visited you again. In fact, you told us not to come. You rarely shared your grades, but you did reassure us that you were doing fine. You found a part-time job at a local restaurant and later told us that you had met your boyfriend.

The two of you began to date, and before we knew it, you had moved in with him. Sean later informed us that he and several friends helped you move in with your boyfriend.

Several months later, you called Sean again and asked him to help you move out. Your boyfriend had physically attacked you. Sean helped you move again and warned you to stay away from that boy.

Sean, when you told us all this, we were worried and unsure how to address the situation, especially since you had reported the information to us in confidence. We were grateful, at least, that you and your sister were close enough to help each other. Later you told us that Lee's boyfriend was trying to win her back.

Letting You Go Requires Courage

A few months later, you said that Lee called you a third time to help her move back in again with the same boyfriend. This time you balked and you pleaded with her not to move back. Eventually, you did help her, because you knew she would somehow move in with her boyfriend anyway.

Lee, this was the beginning of many years of new concern Dad and I had for you as we tried to let you live your own life and make your own decisions, even when we just wanted to swoop in and try to save you from what seemed to us like an unhealthy relationship.

YOUR TURN TO REFLECT

What does "letting go" mean to you as a parent?

What did you do to enable your children to become their own person?

REFLECTION 29

A NIGHTMARE MIGHT HAVE BEEN A BLESSING

Our first difficult moments were in person with your boyfriend when your maternal grandparents flew in from Hawaii to celebrate your college graduation. Unknown to us, you had invited your boyfriend to dinner to introduce him to the family.

At dinner we tried to get to know him by asking about his work, his plans, where he was from, his family … very much the usual parental interview.

I thought it odd that when we asked him about his plans and future he kept saying about you, "This was her idea to move in. She has many ideas that I support. I do what she says." When we asked about his family, he responded, "They are in Mexico. I came here for education as a kid."

I grew increasingly uneasy as it seemed he was avoiding answering any of our questions. It was, however, just our first meeting, and I knew he might have been nervous. You had been excited to introduce him, and we left still curious about your relationship with him.

We were proud of your achievements and happy when you found a well-paying job after college. You and your boyfriend continued to live together, and you eventually got pregnant and had your first child. We flew from Hawaii to meet the new baby, our first grandchild, and we stayed at a hotel because, although we wanted to help you with your newborn, we did not want to invade your privacy. I couldn't understand why you insisted that you didn't need our help, saying you had plenty of support from your boyfriend's family.

We felt awkward and unwelcomed during that visit.

We were worried and confused about why you would live with someone and have a baby with him when he had previously abused you. We rationalized that you were part of a new generation with different morals and values, and you could easily "control the situation of abuse" and even have children without being married. We decided not to interfere with your life choices even though we felt uneasy about your decisions.

It was hard "letting you be," but I believed that was the only way not to trigger your resistance to our advice and to us.

YOUR TURN TO REFLECT

What are some pressing questions that you grapple with as a parent?

How have you answered some, if not all, of them?

REFLECTION 30

SETTING OUR LIMITS HELPED

When Grandma died, you wanted to come to Hawaii for her funeral, so we offered to have you and the baby—not your boyfriend—stay with Grandpa and us. We paid for your airfare. We explained that your grandpa disapproved of unwed couples living together, much less having a baby. We disliked your boyfriend and wanted to be clear that he was not welcome; we were glad we could use Grandpa as an excuse.

If we had told you our feelings, we were afraid you would not come.

You came without your boyfriend, and your grandpa enjoyed the chance to babysit and meet your baby for the first time. Dad and I also enjoyed the baby and, for the first time, you asked me about how to comfort your colicky baby and generally, how to raise a child.

YOUR TURN TO REFLECT

How do you make decisions as a parent so as to teach your child?

REFLECTION 31

WHEN YOUR OPPONENT PUSHES, STEP ASIDE

This is a lesson from martial arts. When your firstborn was five years old, Lee, you and your boyfriend decided to get married and hold the wedding in Hawaii. You said your boyfriend wanted another child, but you wouldn't consent unless you were married. Later, we found out your boyfriend was still married to someone else when you had your first child, so he needed to get divorced first. It disturbed us greatly that your marriage would come about only through a threat over a baby ... or so it seemed.

I thought again, *This must be a new generation, a new culture.* But I wondered, *What have we taught you, anyway?*

Dad and I had moved in with Grandpa by then, and when you asked if we could help you with your wedding, of course, we agreed to help. Your aunt and uncle and family friends were happy to help as well. We were ambivalent about the wedding, though, because we still didn't like your boyfriend and we were concerned about your welfare with him, but we wanted to support your decisions. After all, we realized we didn't have to live with him. You did.

Letting You Go Requires Courage

Dad and I asked you right before the wedding ceremony, "Do you love this man?"

"I think so," you replied.

My heart sank. I silently wept with sorrow. I had to walk away to calm myself for the wedding. Your dad and I knew the wedding was a mistake, but you wouldn't listen to us. You were so invested in that relationship.

We were shocked. I wondered, *What is she thinking? Are she and I so unalike? What has happened to our daughter?* You seemed so distant from us and entrenched in your new husband's family and culture. You dressed, talked, and thought like them, embracing their values. Dad and I felt like you had transformed into another person.

After the wedding, we rarely heard from you. You had a second child and insisted that you didn't need our help. You told us then, "You don't need to come to visit." We came anyway but left after a few days.

Ten years later, Sean told us that you had thought we didn't love you. We were deeply hurt and wondered, *How did this come about?*

We had to figure out a way to convince you, even though we felt cut off from you, that we have always loved you.

Dad had a consulting job near where you lived. He reached out by visiting you one day and he gently told you that, by his observations, you didn't look happy.

"Mind your own business, Dad. You don't know my family, so don't make judgments!"

Dad told me that you had spoken so angrily to him as you pushed back with resistance. He left feeling hurt, upset, and helpless to get through to you.

YOUR TURN TO REFLECT

Did you deliberately step aside as a way to help your child?

If you did, what were the circumstances and the outcomes?

REFLECTION 32

DELIBERATELY CREATING LOVE EXPERIENCES

Dad and I regrouped to figure out another way to reach you. Since we couldn't easily talk with you, we decided to create "love experiences" instead, something we call "catching with honey."

Dad and I had planned on taking a pilgrimage to Minidoka, Idaho, to visit Dad's birthplace and to pay our respect to his parents and the other Japanese-Americans incarcerated there during WW II. We decided to use the trip as a family reunion. We had never been together as a family after you both left for college, so we weren't sure if either of you would come.

Sean, you responded immediately and said, "Sure! Thanks!"

Lee, you didn't respond, so we offered to pay for timeshare rentals and make this trip an adventure for the grandchildren. We offered to book a whitewater river rafting trip for the whole family as well. We thought maybe that would make it easier for you to accept our invitation. You immediately responded that you'd love to come and bring the family, but maybe not stay for all seven days, just four, as you had to get back for work.

We thought you were testing whether we could all get along and wanted an escape route by making it a short trip.

After you arrived at the timeshare condos, we explained to you and your family the history of the Japanese-American internment and, in particular, we told you your grandparents' story. Better late than never, I guessed. We showed you the location of where the camp hospital once stood and where your dad was born, remnants of the guard towers and the entrance where soldiers could shoot anyone trying to escape, and what remained of the concrete foundations where tar-paper-walled barracks housed the prisoners.

We all said silent prayers and left.

"See. You're not the only one who suffered," you told your husband on our drive back to our condos.

When you suggested at the end of the visit that we meet once a year for a reunion, Dad and I rejoiced and silently celebrated.

YOUR TURN TO REFLECT

Did you address challenging situations with actions instead of words as a parenting maneuver?

What did you learn about yourself when you did that?

REFLECTION 33

NEVER GIVE UP—THE TRUTH EMERGES

After that, we planned annual reunions in California, Washington, Hawaii, and Canada. We used our timeshare properties, and each reunion became more extended and enabled us to renew our relationships and expose our grandchildren to more adventures. We saw that the grandchildren seemed afraid to try new things, and we tried to find activities that would teach them new skills and help them learn the powers of observation and self-confidence, just as we had tried to do with the two of you.

Lee, during one reunion in Hawaii, Dad, your husband, your then-fifteen-year-old son, and I were sitting around the swimming pool, talking with other guests staying at the timeshare property. You were still inside your room with your younger son.

Your husband suddenly seemed agitated and, without provocation, pointed at your son and yelled at everyone there.

"See my son? He is a fat nobody!"

"You're the nobody!" your son roared back. "You never finished high school!"

Letting You Go Requires Courage

We were appalled by this outrageous behavior. We wondered when this verbal abuse of your child had begun, and we worried for everyone's safety.

Dad and I told you about what had happened as soon as we were with you alone back inside.

You confided to us that you were thinking of a divorce. We were shocked but secretly grateful for what we felt was divine intervention.

When you did actually file for divorce, we were even more overjoyed.

Your husband never came to another family reunion. After that, we wondered why we were all so relaxed together and having such great times at our reunions. Sean, you hit the nail on the head when you explained why to the rest of us: "Lee's husband isn't here," you said.

Duh, I thought. Sean, you are so observant.

Lee, you told us more about your marriage shortly after your divorce. It broke my heart and saddened me to hear that your husband had convinced you that he was the only one who loved you. You were adopted, he reminded you, so, he said, that proved the fact. He said your biological parents had given you away, and Dad and I had adopted you *out of pity*. He told you that he didn't want us to brainwash his children, so you kept us away with little or no communication.

We learned that he was having affairs, accumulating debt, relying on you to support him financially, and the two of you were constantly arguing and yelling. Sometimes you hit each other. Your children later confirmed that it was difficult for them to concentrate and focus in school. When we learned that your older child was on the verge of failing high school, we tried to encourage and teach him how to learn whenever we saw him. Amazingly, ten years later, he still talks about our sessions on learning.

You never denied the chaos, and you expressed your remorse for putting your children through that nightmare.

I felt close to you again, Lee. Our bond was still there.

YOUR TURN TO REFLECT

What truths have you learned about your children that you never thought would unfold?

REFLECTION 34

LOVE PREVAILS

Several years later, Lee, you quit your high-paying job on the mainland and moved to Hawaii with your younger child. We were surprised that you wanted to be near us and asked us to help raise this second child. Your older child stayed where you'd been living.

We felt blessed for this second opportunity to re-parent you and to begin our grandparenting. You found a dream job and a lovely apartment not far from us, and your child made friends and flourished in school.

I knew that every event now was a miracle unfolding. I thanked God for giving us back our daughter.

In 2007, you told us that your birth mother had found you and contacted you. You corresponded with each other for many years afterward and, in 2019, you and your younger son flew to Korea to meet your birth family. I knew you needed to reconnect with your birth mother, learn about your history there, and find your identity with them. Dad and I were excited for you. We strongly supported the trip and gave you gifts to give your birth family.

Lee, I no longer worry about you. I can just focus on loving you and your sons. In the long process of our bonding, I have learned to forgive myself for not intervening in your marriage and trying to "save" you. Dad keeps reminding you it's about seeing the inside of a person, not the outside. I have finally found great peace. I now know that I can only be a beacon to you and shine a light for you to see your way through life your way ... in your own time.

Always with Much Love and Deep Aloha,
Mom

YOUR TURN TO REFLECT

What miracles of love have unfolded for you as a parent? Recall the humorous and joyful moments of raising children.

_____
_____
_____
_____
_____
_____

What do these moments tell you about you and your parenting style?

_____
_____
_____
_____
_____
_____
_____

PART FIVE

MY CHILDREN HAVE TAUGHT ME MORE THAN I HAVE TAUGHT THEM

Do not conquer the world by force, for force only causes resistance.

Lao Tzu

MY TRANSFORMATION

Dearest Sean and Lee,
Your lives have transformed me.

Because of you, I have learned to love without conditions or expectations, and I have stepped back so that you could live your lives. I had to trust that you—on your own or with our help—would develop the skills and values to give you the confidence to move through life.

The miracle has not been that you have changed into people like Dad and me, people with our values. The gift I have come to learn is that we have loved you no matter what.

Love is the true miracle.

Otherwise, how could we have survived as a family?

As parents, we wanted you to find the confidence to live in your Spirit. Self-confidence translates to self-love.

In retrospect, Dad and I now see that our task was to help you know your strengths, support your journeys, and love you no matter what.

Now that we are in our golden years, you selectively tell us what you do. That's fine. It is incredible to watch as you care for the elderly and respect your own ancestors by visiting the family gravesite whenever possible. You look forward to seeing your cousins. You are kind to each other, and you freely help others, as well. Sean, I watch you study and use *Ho'oponopono*, the Hawaiian protocol of forgiveness, in your relationships and your life.

You are both living the values we had hoped to teach you, but each of you live them in your own unique way.

For me, the parenting journey was like watching two flowers unfold from the same plant and discovering that no two flowers are alike.

YOUR TURN TO REFLECT

If you could tell your children about your experience of living and growing together, what would you tell them?

HAVE COMPASSION FOR YOURSELF AS A PARENT

Perhaps the biggest lesson I have learned is to know that as a parent, I have been enough.

Recognizing that, I have learned to have compassion for my own mistakes and to reframe those mistakes as reflections. I have learned that children forgive and that the best things we can do for our children are to let go of our egos, find the humility to know that we do not know everything all the time, have the courage to change ourselves, and never give up.

After twenty years of schooling, obtaining a PhD in psychology and a master's degree in family counseling, armed with years of theories and successful stories, I have learned that I could not be—and never was—completely in control of any situation in our family.

I saw that the more effort I put into trying to be in control, the less in control I was.

I became so embarrassed at one point as a therapist and parent and felt so defeated by my failures that I almost left the field of Western psychology for good. I was truly humiliated and thought I had failed as a parent.

I wondered why I had thought I could ever help anyone in the first place.

In my study of the Eastern philosophy of my ancestors, I finally received the help I needed. For whatever divine reason, I had been forced to stop pushing against you, my children, and against the Western values I had tried so hard to make part of my identity.

In my new studies, I learned about *wu-wei* (meaning "effortless action") and through that truth, I recognized why I failed. The Taoist principle of *wu-wei* explains that problems are created in human relationships by resisting what we don't like in others—just as I had done with you, Sean and Lee. It offers the wisdom of another way. *Wu-wei* is about "not forcing"; it is about going with the flow, and knowing how and when to take the line of least resistance in one's actions. It stresses a harmonious and nonaggressive yet active approach toward others, which ultimately leads to happiness for all. I was taught to be like bamboo; it grows stronger when it bends with the wind.

That practical philosophy has allowed me to successfully challenge my earlier theories and rethink—and then readjust—what I was doing. I could then recognize that you children had been trying to teach me that true growth was about learning to grow in confidence about my own life ... so that I could then be confident in yours. I needed to bend to make you strong.

I learned that I had to trust you if you were going to survive and if you were going to learn how to live in your own spirit.

After thirty years of pushing each other away, we are now all back together. You both are close to Dad and me ... in your own ways, of course.

From my years of meditation and my study of the Tao, I have finally learned that we find peace and joy within ourselves first. Only then can we attract what we seek to influence our environment. And, if we don't get what we desire, that's okay. The universe may have a bigger—or at least a different—plan for us.

Because of you, my dear children, I am better at caring for myself and at letting others walk their own paths.

That is the miracle of parenting.

Always with Much Love and Deep Aloha,
Mom

YOUR TURN TO REFLECT

Write a letter to yourself about your parenting journey. Include all the moments of joy, surprise, and enchantment.

ACKNOWLEDGMENTS

Writing doesn't come easily for me, yet with a cheering squad of folks, I couldn't help but finish. First and foremost, a big thanks to Ken, my husband, who encouraged me and kept me focused, and to my children who allowed me to tell our story. All you asked is that I tell the truth. I thank you for your love, support, and encouragement.

Thanks to Rob Carr for helping me turn random thoughts into book form. A big thank you to Nina Shoroplova and Geoff Affleck for their wisdom, guidance, gentle editing, and patience in the production of this book. You both were wonderful mentors who encouraged me and showed me how to complete this book. Finally, my heartfelt thank you to my dear friends who critically reviewed the manuscript to make it even better.

My deepest appreciation to you all. *Mahalo nui loa kakou* (Hawaiian for "a heartfelt thank you to you all").

Ann S. Yabusaki

ABOUT THE AUTHOR

Ann S. Yabusaki, PhD, is a family therapist and psychologist. She has counseled many individuals and families, letting go of counseling theories and strategies and, instead, aligning with Unconditional Love. She counsels people about Unconditional Love as patience, deep listening, self-compassion, laughter, and letting go.

Dr. Ann welcomes your comments and reflections. Please contact her at Ayabusaki2@gmail.com.

Made in United States
North Haven, CT
28 April 2023